BLACK ELK

BLACK ELK

The Sacred Ways of a Lakota

WALLACE H. BLACK ELK
AND
WILLIAM S. LYON, PH.D.

1817

Harper & Row, Publishers, San Francisco

New York, Grand Rapids, Philadelphia, St. Louis
London, Singapore, Sydney, Tokyo, Toronto

FIRST EDITION

Library of Congress Cataloging-in-Publication Data
Black Elk, Wallace H.
  Black Elk: the sacred powers of a Lakota
Wallace H. Black Elk and William S. Lyon.—1st ed.
  p.   cm.
  ISBN 0-06-250523-8
  1. Oglala Indians—Religion and mythology. 2. Shamanism—Colorado. 3. Black Elk, Wallace H.   I. Lyon, William S., Ph.D.
II. Title.
E99.O3B48   1990   89-45563
299'.785—dc20   CIP

---

90 91 92 93 94 RINAM 10 9 8 7 6 5 4 3 2 1

IHO

Tunkaŝila, unci maka wamakanŝkanya
tatuye topa kin lena tawaic'iya nanke.
Na maka wita kin le, cannunpa kin le,
ikce wicaŝa hena unkawanlakapi,
wicouncaġe topa kin lena wicotakuniŝni
hinajinpi eŝa hena kakuŝyeya najin yo!

Tunkaŝila, unŝimala yo!

Ohunkeŝni na wakanyeja hena iyuŝkinya,
zaniya manipi kte.

Wokiye kaġa yo!

Taku wakan ecetkiya hounkiciciya po! Mitakuye ob
takuni itokeca kte ŝni.

Mazani kte! Wani kte!

Tunkaŝila, hoiciciyelo

Unŝimala yo! Omakiya yo!

Mitakuye Oyas'in
Wanbli cik'ala

Dedication Prayer

Grandfather,
Grandmother,

to the Powers in the Animal Nations
of the Four Winds.
Watch over
the Chanunpa, Grandmother Earth,
and the People:
Our Forefathers, Elders,
Little Ones,
and the Unborn.

Tunkashila,
have pity on me.
I pray through the Chanunpa
for my People, all life,
for health and happiness.
Grandfather,
Grandmother,
hear my prayer.
I humble myself,
help me.
This is me
Wanbli cik'ala.

Mitakuye Oyas'in

I dedicate this book to the People, the Elders, and the Unborn:

. . . of the Black Nation
. . . of the Red Nation
. . . of the Yellow Nation
. . . of the White Nation
. . . of the Animal Spirits
. . . of the Four Winds
. . . of the Spotted Eagle Nation
. . . and of the Mole Nation

I wish to commemorate my Forefathers who courageously carried the Chanunpa and who prayed for us: The Hornchips and The Moves Camp.

This dedication is for:

Our People who courageously laid down their Robes to keep our Sacred Rites alive, and all the People who passed on to the Spirit World.
The Keepers of the Chanunpa: Stanley and Orville Looking Horse and Families.

All the Chanunpa Carriers.
All Our People.
My Family.

The Stone People, the Medicine People, The Fire Generation.
And for Our Grandmother Earth and Tunkashila.

Special thanks to Bernard Ice, Cindy Chadwick, Bob Tichy, and
Calvin Fast Wolf for their help in the transcription of this
dedication.

W.B.E.

To my daughter, April Cybelle Lyon,
who has always been there for me.

W. S. L.

Contents

Preface

Since our earliest contacts with the first inhabitants of North America, nothing has been more intriguing to the Western mind than the sacred mystery powers of the Native American shamans (medicine men). Although shamans have appeared in some form in nearly every culture throughout history, we still know very little about their remarkable powers. What we have learned from our studies of shamanism is that its core resides deep within the human psyche. Shamanism involves the ability to enter into an altered state of consciousness *at will* in order to acquire help from spirits. Both the spirits and their aid are manifested mysteriously. One never knows which spirit is going to "jump in" or what it will do. The spirits seem to come of their own volition, yet once a spirit appears to a shaman, the shaman is said to have "caught" that spirit, and a spirit that has been "caught" can, in turn, be recalled at any time by that shaman. The actual rituals or techniques used to do this usually differ from shaman to shaman because, most often, such instructions come directly from the spirits to the shaman. Frequently the shaman receives a sacred song—a spirit-calling song—to be sung for this purpose.

North American shamanism is unique in that it has remained relatively untouched by any of the major world religions. This is not the case for the shamans of Europe, Asia, or Africa, where shamanism often takes on Taoist, Christian, or Buddhist motifs. In North America, however, shamanism has remained basically the same for thousands of years. The Native American form of shamanism, rooted deeply in nature and natural elements, is perhaps one of the most pure and powerful forms of shamanism in existence today. It has survived (perhaps barely) the onslaught of industrialized civilization and the persecutions of church and state. Still, very few authentic shamans remain. Most of them are hidden from our view, scattered along the back roads of reservations across this land. With few concerns for the outside world, they quietly and humbly serve those who come begging them for aid. From the viewpoint of the psychology of consciousness, shamans are master technicians at altered states of consciousness. We should protect these elusive and shy professionals as we do our most endangered species. They are the guardians of a rare, but once powerful, force in humankind. The forces they are able to tap, we little understand. Yet, if we are to survive such threats as AIDS, nuclear waste, and the greenhouse effect, it would be naive of us not to seek their assistance.

It was Carlos Castaneda's fanciful sprints through shaman-land with Don Juan that, by the 1970s, first brought about a widespread interest in shamanism. Although Don Juan was more sorcerer than shaman, such concepts of power were new to us. His reported adventures seemed somewhere between fantasy and intrigue. To Native American elders, such narratives were neither new nor very interesting, nor did they believe that anyone would really want to live the life of a shaman. Shamanic training requires a great deal of personal suffering, social isolation, and the psychological fortitude to withstand great terror. It takes years to master the ability to self-induce a trance at will; just to reach the first Lakota "level of power" often takes around sixteen years of training in self-control. The most powerful shamans often lead solitary lives full of arduous service with few personal rewards. Those shamans who do marry often fear for the safety of their children. Because their powers always manifest themselves on the wings of mystery, shamans are more likely to be suspected than respected. Finally, there is no graduation from the school of shamanism, for it is more a way of life than a school of techniques for effecting magic.

In 1978, the Native American Religious Freedom Act was signed into law. It was the response of Congress to public pressures (brought about by such events as the occupation of Wounded Knee) to stop the suppression of Native American traditions. The passage of this law encouraged traditional shamans to come out of hiding. Today, such shamans as Rolling Thunder, Fools Crow, and Lame Deer are well known. However, earlier in this century, especially during the 1920s and 1930s, most shamans had to practice in secret. One of the major exceptions was Nicholas Black Elk, a Lakota shaman whose story was told by John Neihardt in *Black Elk Speaks* (1932) and again in Joseph Epes Brown's *The Sacred Pipe* (1953). These two books form one of the most penetrating views to date of what North American shamanism is all about.

According to Neihardt, Nick was attempting "to save his Great Vision for men" (*Black Elk Speaks,* 1960 ed., p. xi), which meant saving the shamanic lineage, or in Black Elk's own words, seeing the Tree of Life bloom again. Nearly two decades later and near death in 1948, Black Elk collaborated with Joseph Brown because "he did not wish that this sacred lore, much of which he alone knew, should pass with him" (*The Sacred Pipe,* p. x).

John Neihardt, a poet, focused primarily on the visionary aspects of Black Elk's shamanism, while Brown wrote about the seven major Lakota rituals. Both writers together give a deep insight into Black Elk's personality and his views on shamanism, but they tell virtually nothing regarding his practice thereof. In fact, many scholars believe Black Elk stopped his shamanic practice around 1904, when he was baptized a Catholic. I have reason to believe he continued on in secret.

Following Brown's book, there was a twenty-year silence. Then, in 1972, Richard Erdoes published *Lame Deer: Seeker of Visions,* which was followed by Thomas Mails's *Fools Crow* in 1979. As autobiographical accounts, these two books do not hold to the subject of shamanism exclusively. However, many new insights into Lakota shamanism were gained from these works.

We now have a rare opportunity to penetrate even deeper into the core of Lakota shamanism, this time through the words of Wallace Black Elk, also a renowned Lakota shaman. In fact, such a detailed account of Native American shamanism by a practicing shaman has never before been compiled for general reading. What Nick Black Elk failed to do in his lifetime, Wallace Black Elk attempts to achieve in his—to bring the sacred mystery powers back into the hands of the people and to see the Tree of Life bloom again on Earth. Wallace, however, extends his scope beyond the realm of the Lakota Nation to include all human beings. He believes that the power of the Sacred Pipe is for everyone. Wallace noted long ago that when the spirits do appear, they never lay claim to a racial identity. In fact, Lakota prophecy speaks of the Sacred Pipe as going out to all nations. Shamans need only follow the sacred rules for handling (carrying) a Sacred Pipe. From his perspective, we would all be better off if we each received some personal guidance in our life through direct communication with a "guardian angel." Wallace's attitude may irritate those who think whites are stealing the Indian's religion, but he sees this worldview as not simply his personal philosophy but as part of the sacred teachings themselves. In his Earth People philosophy, power is seen as a gift from the Creator for all human beings.

I first met Wallace Black Elk in the summer of 1978 through a friend named Charles Cameron. Charles was an Oxford-educated poet who was a colleague at the small college in southern Oregon where I worked. We were both very interested in creative teaching methods and were involved in a new "living-learning" program being tested by the school. Charles personally knew Wallace from an earlier stay in Denver, where Black Elk lives, and he suggested that it might be worthwhile to involve him in the new program. The anthropologist in me had no problem with the thought of meeting a very much alive shaman. By then, I had been studying Native Americans for over a decade, but mostly from books. Armed with purpose, I convinced our summer session director that a two-week course at the end of the summer session that included a Native American shaman might boost his enrollments—and it did.

On a hot, August afternoon in 1978, about fifty students gathered in a basement classroom for what was about to become the first of many adventures I had with Black Elk. On that first afternoon I was clearly in unfamiliar territory. I explained to the students that Black Elk and I had decided that the subject matter of the course was to be the first step in most Lakota rituals, known as the *inipi* ceremony—purification by sweating, singing, and praying. Black Elk translates this into English as the "stone-people-lodge" ceremony. We selected it because, historically, it is the most widespread Native American purification ceremony ever used, and, as such, it is also the most common ceremony found in North America. The purification of self is the first step in any major sacred undertaking, regardless of time and culture. Therefore, no ceremony is more basic to all Native American cultures than this one. It was their universal starting point.

After finishing my introductory remarks, out of respect for Black Elk I turned the class over for comments and questions. At one point a female student raised her hand and asked, "Mr. Black Elk, exactly what do we wear in the sweat-lodge?" With stoic face and dignified authority, Black Elk immediately replied, "You wear that suit you were born in—that birthday suit." He had not spoken the whole truth. Not only were traditional Native Americans usually very sensitive to nudity, but among the Lakota, men and women usually went into separate lodges. Some students began to squirm in their seats, for Black Elk had already begun the teaching process.

By eight o'clock the next morning I found myself standing before an anxious dean who was explaining to me that the father of one of my students was about to bring suit against the college because his daughter had to appear naked in public to earn a grade in my class. I told Black Elk that we were in big trouble, but he merely looked at me, smiled, and said, "Don't worry. It will be okay." "Easy for him to say," I thought at the time. Three months later, when our college won a national award for creativity with that very class, the dean had a smile on his face when he flew to the Midwest to accept the award on behalf of the college. Everything was "okay" from then on, and Black Elk returned each year thereafter.

Around 1983, Wallace suggested that I quit teaching and assist him as a "translator." From our perspective, the stakes were high—access to uncharted knowledge of shamanism versus my job. After two years of considerable introspection, I opted for adventure and resigned my tenured professorship. Since Wallace speaks English, one might wonder why a translator is needed. The reason is this: Wallace thinks in Lakota and translates, as he speaks, directly into English. For Wallace, if you don't think in English, you don't speak it. That is why he often says, "I don't speak English." Also, the organization of his thoughts follows the Lakota pattern of making a point from many different angles, in contrast to our style of holding to one subject. Therefore, when you hear him speak, his thoughts seem to circle about. He drifts along, and, if you don't sense the point being made, you often wonder what he is talking about. The real gap, however, is not so much between the Lakota and English languages as between sacred and profane levels of being. In Black Elk's world, spirits are more real than matter.

We live in a world nearly devoid of the sacred mystery powers that once abounded via shamans throughout humankind. It is difficult for us to imagine that perhaps we could all use a little magic in our lives. Our thoughts convince us that magic is impossible or, at best, only an illusion. That's where "translation" comes in. Quite frankly, our assumptions about the basic nature of reality are, in this regard, false. Medicine men do cause unbelievable things to occur, but what makes their feats seem so "unbelievable" to us is that we have yet to believe that time is, for certain, a relative affair. Shamans know that to be a fact. In that sense, they are advanced physicists, and with proper "translation" I am sure they have a few things to tell us about the "laws of nature." After all, from Black Elk's perspective, shamanism is the original technology and science.

This book, then, is an attempt at translation. The first question will be, "Did Black Elk really say the things written here?" In answering that question, let me briefly compare this book with Neihardt's, since they complement each other. In *Black Elk Speaks,* Neihardt freely admitted to authoring both the first and last chapters of the book. Furthermore, it was Neihardt's daughter, Enid, who actually took, in shorthand, the field notes from which the book was created. What she wrote down was the English narration she heard from Ben Black Elk, who was translating from Lakota what Nick was saying. Later on, she rewrote her notes into longhand for her father to use in his writing of the book. My process with Wallace Black Elk has been much different. All of the material used in this book was taken from tape-recorded sessions during which Wallace spoke in English. In reviewing these tapes for this book, I transcribed, for the most part, only the material that in some way related to Black Elk's practice of shamanism. Essentially, then, there is nothing written here that you could not also hear Black Elk saying at some point on one of these recorded tapes. Given these differences in approach, I consider Wallace's words here to be more accurate with regard to his personal understandings of the sacred mystery powers than any of the material written in the name of Nick Black Elk. That is to say, I believe there is less interference found here between the actual spoken words of Wallace and my work as translator than in any of the material by Nick.

As "translator," I made two major alterations in the material as recorded on tape. The first was to edit together into one single account disparate parts of the same story, especially with regard to accounts of visionary experiences. Recall that Wallace does not organize his thought processes as we do. For example, he is much more likely to tell only a single aspect of one of his visionary experiences, in order to make a certain point, than he is to cover an entire visionary experience during the course of one conversation. To tell one's visionary experience in its entirety is a sacred undertaking that is done in the stone-people-lodge right after the completion of a vision quest. It would never seem appropriate to him to render a full account of a vision under any other circumstances. Accordingly, differing accounts were compared in order to enrich the material—to give the reader access to more recorded details.

Second, I have altered Wallace's grammar to conform, for the most part, to our standards. As noted earlier, when speaking, he is thinking in Lakota while he translates directly into English. Since the Lakota word order is different from ours, his English often sounds "backwards" to our ears. This makes his English often sound "incorrect." These alterations were made, therefore, to free the reader from having continually to say, "Oh, he must mean . . ." They simply make for smoother reading.

In addition, I have made other, minor alterations in the material as recorded. For instance, I have removed most personal idiosyncrasies from the tapes, such as long hesitations between sentences, repetitions of the same word or phrase, misuse of a word followed by its corrected usage, mispronunciation, etc. Also, in order to make the transition from one topic to another, I have added, now and then, a transitional sentence to the original material, such as, "One time we were at . . . ," or, "I can remember when . . ." These minor alterations were also introduced to make the text flow more smoothly.

In moving the material from tape to page, my foremost concern was to preserve Black Elk's original intent. For example, Black Elk often uses the term *Pipe* or *Pipe ceremony* when referring to the Sacred Pipe. However, Black Elk prefers the Lakota word for the Sacred Pipe, which is *Chanunpa*. Therefore, in transcribing the material from tapes, I most often substituted the term *Chanunpa* for *Pipe* in order to give a more exact "translation." Given over a decade of working with Wallace, I feel that this book contains about as true and accurate a picture of his views as one could possibly present, at least in English and without extensive additions. Nevertheless, just to keep Black Elk's essence alive in the narrative, I have also included some material that even I do not clearly understand. Therefore, please expect not to understand everything he says.

The first half of the book covers, for the most part, Black Elk's early training as a shaman. His training was unique in several respects. Traditionally, most shamans receive an "initiatory call." This "call" is seen as accidental, since it most often comes during a personal illness serious enough to induce a coma (a form of trance). Such was the case with Nick Black Elk, who lay in a coma for twelve days at age nine only to experience his life-altering "Great Vision." In fact, his vision was so overwhelming to him that it took him seven years thereafter to realize he had any real power or even to speak to anyone about it, for fear of being thought foolish. Wallace's initiatory call was preplanned. His tribal elders introduced him (via ritual) to the spirits when he was only five years old. This is rare, since in most cultures, shamanic training does not begin until after the onset of puberty; shamanism is for adults, not children. Wallace's induction occurred around 1926, a period in which the elders were certainly very much in fear of losing their shamanic lineages. From their perspective, the ability of their shamans to tap into the sacred mystery powers was their most-valued knowledge. To lose their shamanic powers was surely seen as tantamount to the death of the "old ways," and rightfully so.

Wallace Black Elk's shamanic training was also unique in that he had so many "grandfathers" involved in teaching him the "red road" (spiritual life-style). Normally, an upcoming shaman will train under only one mentor. It is really the function of the teacher to train the novice how to be trained directly by the spirits. That is, the advanced instructions normally come from the spirits themselves. Wallace, however, reports that he had eleven "grandfathers" who assisted in his early training, one of whom was Nick Black Elk. There was something else unique about Wallace. He was the first in his family to learn English. Wallace remembers that between the ages of five and nine he was taught by the spirits "all the [English] terminologies used in the universities today." Although such a feat is incomprehensible to us, the elders must have noted his remarkable command of English. This observation probably caused them to focus even more attention on his initial training. They may even have seen this ability as a prophetic sign. Whatever the reasons, Wallace's training was not routine. In addition, he is now entering his sixty-fourth year of training. To date he has completed over thirty vision quests, and he plans for more powerful ones to come. Because of all these factors, I hold him to be one of the truly great shamans of our time.

The second half of the book centers on Black Elk's applications of the sacred mystery powers. He states that power comes for two purposes—health and help (or, more recently, happiness). That covers a vast range of human needs, and it is here that readers will begin to sense the nature of power inherent in shamanism. For the Lakota shamans who believe in and use the spirits, sacred power seemingly has no limits. What may seem unusual, even paranormal to us, is an everyday part of their world. They do not question the existence of power, only its application. That is a universal concern among shamans. An African anthropologist once told me about his taking a famous psychic to visit the Bushmen shamans of South Africa. The psychic demonstrated for them his ability to bend spoons with his mind. They only laughed, asking if that was all that he knew how to do with his power. Readers may find the second part of the book unbelievable in many respects, but to laugh it away is to give the shamans the last laugh.

I want to say something about how Wallace Black Elk is related to Nick Black Elk. Some people may believe that one's genes can determine one's shamanic abilities. I don't believe that, and so I was never concerned enough to establish their distant blood relationship if any at all. Both of them spell their Lakota name the same—*Hehake sapa. Hehake* is Lakota for the male elk, and *sapa* means "black." (Wallace, however, has said that his name had been mistranslated. Instead of an elk black in color, originally his name in Lakota meant the "black elk" as seen in the silhouetted figure of an elk at early sunrise or late sunset.) Whenever Wallace does refer to Nick, he refers to him as "my grandfather," but Nick was not Wallace's biological grandfather. Wallace had eleven "grandfathers." Wallace and Nick's real relationship, then, is a spiritual one within the Lakota shamanic tradition. They both first encountered spirits at the age of five, and they both had their first visionary experience at the age of nine. On that level they are very much related. Indeed, so much so, that Wallace will say that they still speak to one another.

Finally, a few words about myself and this work. This book is designed to cover a broad range of interests. It may be used for entertainment, instruction, or scholarly purposes. It has been ten years in the making and one year in writing. Black Elk still says that I need to be more patient. I published my first professional paper on Native Americans in 1963. It was a technical report on the physical features of a female Indian skull. Black Elk never knew that, but the spirits did. In 1986, the spirits told Wallace my secret in the course of giving me a sacred name—*Hohu sha,* meaning "red bone." They do seem to have a good sense of humor.

What began in 1978 as a small class on the *inipi* ceremony with Black Elk has now become a large, annual Sun Dance in the same locale. There is no doubt that over the years our endearment to each other has matured. He has adopted me as his nephew, and, in turn, I call him *lekshi,* the Lakota word for "uncle." I'm still a professional anthropologist and not a shaman. Yet I have my feet in both worlds. It is difficult to keep such a balance, for one is all too likely to be misunderstood both on one side and the other. But it turns out there is really only one side; it is our perspective on things that makes it appear as duality. After eleven years of participating in sacred ceremonies and listening to Black Elk, I finally carved my own Sacred Pipe and went on my first vision quest. My goal is to complete four annual quests in succession. That is under way. There are things I now know about shamanism that shall never be put into writing. If ever I catch a spirit . . .

WILLIAM S. LYON

Acknowledgments

To Charles Cameron of Los Angeles, for first introducing me to Wallace Black Elk.

To Dr. Ruth-Inge Heinze of Berkeley, California, for being motivator par excellence throughout the entire undertaking.

To Chrystal Davis of Placerville, Colorado, for providing me a sanctuary in which to transcribe the Black Elk tapes, and for her lifelong love of the Red Nation.

To Barbara Todd Kennedy of Atherton, California, for providing me a peace-filled sanctuary in which to compile the manuscript.

To Dr. David and Sharon Balfour of Northridge, California, for being the pillars of emotional stability every time the ground got shaky.

To Dr. E. Theodore Lechner of Lawton, Oklahoma, for his very extensive reviewing of and commentary on the manuscript.

To Paula White McElmury of Canoga Park, California, and Wesley A. Black Elk of Carson City, Nevada, for their reading of the manuscript and personal commentary.

To Joan Halifax of Ojai Foundation, Ojai, California, for her valuable insights.

To Prof. Alan Dundes of the University of California, Berkeley, for supporting the required research.

To Mato and Lynda Snodgrass, and Ed and Joan Hertzberg, all of Ashland, Oregon, for special advice and support beyond the call of duty.

To the staff of Harper & Row for bending over backwards.

ACKNOWLEDGMENTS

To my many fond friends, here unmentioned, who wished well for this undertaking in many different ways.

And last, and most important, to Wallace Black Elk for being the kindest and most patient human being I have ever known.

BLACK ELK

Part 1

THE MAKING
OF A SHAMAN

CHAPTER 1

The Old Ones

You know, straight across the board, hardly anyone really knows what is Indian. The word *Indian* in itself really doesn't mean anything. That's how come nobody knows anything about Indians. So I want to tell you how I grew up and who I am. I've never read books. I wasn't educated that way. What I am saying here is based on my life. That's what I am telling you. I grew up with this *Chanunpa,** this "Sacred Pipe," and I have a spirit guide with me all the time. He leads me in and out of all the difficulties, all the obstacles I have to go through. The spirit always finds a pathway. The Chanunpa [Sacred Pipe] finds a pathway. It's like a deer trail. If you find a deer trail and follow that trail, it's going to lead you to medicines and waterholes and a shelter.

I began when I was five years old. That sacred power was given to me. It belonged to my forefathers and foremothers. My grandfather and grandmother decided they wanted to leave something with our people so that in future times there would be little guys behind me. So it was for the unborn to come, and we had a prophecy about that nineteen generations before. We can't remember back any further than that. Every seven generations we have a family reunion. You call our family the Sioux, but we call ourselves *Lakota.* We are *Earth People* because we live close to

---

*[Editor's note: Terms defined in the glossary are printed in italics when they first appear in the text.]

our mother, the Earth. At first we all spoke the same language and the same mind. At the end of seven generations we had a big family reunion, and we spoke many different languages. Then everybody went off again. They went in all directions. At the end of that seven generations we had a family reunion, and we spoke even more languages. Each time our people came together they had to unanimously understand where we came from. They had to understand that we are a part of the fire and a part of the rock, or earth, and a part of the water and a part of the green, or living. That way we were able to communicate with all the living. And so we spoke many different languages, but we still spoke the same mind. So we know where we came from. We still know our roots.

At that time we were warned that an unknown power would come to us and would cause in us that little shadow of a doubt. That shadow of a doubt would lead to nothing but hurt and destruction and even to death. For us, death means you are gone forever. For the white man, death means physical death, but to us that is a sleep. In the real death, the spirit is gone forever.

So I learned all this little bitty, kindergarten stuff when I was five years old. We have a biological father and mother, but our real Father is *Tunkashila* [Creator], and our real Mother is the Earth. They give birth and life to all the living, so we know we're all interrelated. We all have the same Father and Mother. That is why you hear us always saying *mitakuye oyasin*. We say those words as we enter the sacred *stone-people-lodge* [sweat-lodge] and also at the end of every prayer. It means "all my relations." It helps to remind us that we are related to everything that exists. So I was educated that way, and it was prophesied nineteen generations ago that that gift would be given to me at the age of five. The old people were waiting and ready for me. So when I was five years old, I became an adult. I was just a little guy, but in my mind I was an adult.

When my old people talked, I always sat right in the middle. I was just a little guy, you know, but I listened to them. It's really hard to hear an old man talk. You have to have a lot of patience to hear those people talk, because when they talk, they talk about the motivation, the feeling, the unsound that is around in the universe. They explain everything to one understanding. They bring it all together, and when they finish, just one word comes out. Just one word. They might talk all day, and just one word comes out. The next day they'll talk again, and then another word comes out. So for three or four days of talking, there might be just three or four words that come out. But once you hear that one word, you hear it and understand it. You'll never forget it because your subconscious mind will see and understand it. That silent communication will come in, and you will receive it. One side of the hemisphere will receive it, and the other side will record it. It will remain with you for the rest of your life. It will go even further to your generation, and generation after generation. It will even go to four generations. So that is really hard for this society here to really understand.

So you have a little tape recorder back there in the mind. I call it color TV, and it records. So if you turn up the volume, the electrical power will come in and hit those little water bubbles or molecules and make a sound. If you turn it down, you could have silence. So that's the way my mind works. So I used to sit there with the old people and turn on my video. Then I would go to sleep, and it would record. So while I was sleeping, the electrical power would come in. It records, runs my heart, pumps my breathing, keeps me living. So when I went there and turned on my video and went to sleep, I could still hear, because this was a spiritual power that came from the wisdom given to us by the Creator and *Grandmother* the Earth.

That power is here all the time. It is continuous, and nobody controls it. The government doesn't control it, and the *BIA* [Bureau of Indian Affairs] doesn't control it. It's continuous, and it just goes on. So that's the way it was with me. I sat there and listened as the old people brought all these powers around. And when you understood, just one word came out—a sacred word. Then I gathered this and the definition, the motivation, the feeling, the unsound came in. I could close my eyes, but I could see little moving pictures. I could see molecules that are like little soap bubbles, and I could see those genes and organics. Then a word comes out. Then that is recorded. So I don't have to write it down here and then file it over here, see? At the same time, I never discovered anything. I don't like that word *discover.* My people—I call them Earth People—never discovered anything, because we are part of the fire, and we're part of the rock, and we're part of the water and green, see? So we never discovered anything or created anything, because we are a part of it. We know we are a part of it, because we are still connected to our roots.

So when I was a little boy, I loved listening to my old people. The other little guys would go out and play around together, but I would go sit with the old people and listen to them. My grandmother and grandpa, they noticed this, so they prayed for me. When they were getting ready for a ceremony, they would give me a little *tobacco tie* [prayer offering] or a piece of sage or cedar. "Here, you could have that." So they made those little offerings to me. So that is the way of the spirit. My forefathers saw it a long time ago. So now, here they picked me, this little guy, this little shrimp, this little rascal. "You could have that." So I'm just a little tobacco tie. I'm just an offering. But my brothers and sisters, they're all good looking. They are all the first-born daughters and first-born sons, so they already have the star place. They are the first ones to eat at the table. What's left over, I eat. When I come home, there's a woodpile. So that's where I sleep. But when I visit my grandma and grandpa, they get up early, so I crawl in their bed. I lie there, and it's warm. Go to sleep. When it's time to eat, they are cooking. "Get up, you're going to eat." So I was the first one to eat. So when I stayed there, I was the first one to eat.

Then, when I was five years old, my grandparents prayed to Tunkashila that I would be given something to hang onto that would help the people behind me, the little ones and the unborn to come. So they put up a ceremony for me and prayed. I was sitting there between Grandma and Mom, and Grandpa was performing this ceremony. When we turned out the lights, those spirits started coming right through the ceiling, and I could see lightning. They came dancing around the room, and each time they hit, there's a lightning, lights. When those spirits came dancing by in front of me, I was pretending like trying to catch them. I wasn't going to catch them, just kind of grabbing at them in the darkness. Then one of them hit me on the forehead. So I tried to catch that one. About that time another one came and hit me on the shoulder, so I tried to catch that one, too. Then another one hit me on the back, but there's a wall there, and I'm leaning against it. Still it hit me on the back like there wasn't anything there.

Those spirits also came as gourds. Those gourds were going around the room rattling. Then one of those gourds came up my pant leg and went out through my shirt sleeve. I tried to catch him also. They were playing with me that way. They were demonstrating to me what they could do. Then two separate gourds came over, and a pair of hands grabbed my wrists, and another pair of hands grabbed my ankles. I thought they were gourds, but they were hands. They lifted me up and started swinging me, and at the same time another pair of hands started tickling me. You know, they call me a dumb Indian, and I must be dumb, because if I had had any sense I would have been screaming, "Mama! Mama!" like that. Instead, I was laughing and kicking around.

Then those spirits started swinging me back and forth and threw me across the room in the dark. Another pair of hands caught me. They tickled me and threw me back. They kept doing that, and on the fourth throw they threw me right through the ceiling. I sailed through that ceiling right out into the solar system. Now that's scary! I could see all those stars around me, and they were showing me the powers of the universe. There was the Creator with his wisdom, and below was the knowledge [of Grandmother the Earth]. So there was a man standing there, and there was a fire there. There was some water there, and this eagle was standing there on this *altar.* Each time it lifted its wing there was a fire underneath it. When he pushed his wing down, there was a tremendous force of wind, like a jet flying through the stratosphere. Hot and cold air hit and vapor. It was something like that. Then it spiraled clockwise, and at the center the sun was sitting right in the middle. And right on the edge, this rock, this Earth, was sitting there. And there were seven stones [planets], like a little race track, going around.

Then the spirit said, "When you return to Earth, tell your people to love each other and stay behind this sacred Chanunpa for there is something moving up there now." That's what he said. So then they brought me back. It was like a jet with rushing and whistling sounds. When they brought me back to the altar there was a wind. There were low clouds and a storm. All my people were there. There was like a moonlight and like a shadow there. The house and floor were gone, and I was standing out in the open. All around me tall grass and weeds were blowing. My people were still there, and I was able to talk to them, but they were all like shadows, little shadows of my ancestors. So I knew they will eventually die. They will lay down their *robe,* and their body will be earth again. There will be weeds, grass, and flowers growing there. But I knew that I would still be able to communicate with my grandma, grandpa, dad, mom, and relatives. So I was really fortunate that I lost nothing.

Then I knew that that altar was the universe, the Earth; that little patch of dirt was the Earth; that little patch of dirt I had seen from out in the universe was this Earth; and that when I left I would still be able to talk to my people, but they would be like shadows. Also, I realized that this power was not something to be toyed around with. So after I came back, I told my people what I had learned from the spirits.

So I'm happy that that vision was given to us when I was just a little guy. After that my grandpa and grandma kept telling me to stay right there where the lodge was. "Don't go away. Don't go away. Stay here. Stay here." For ordinary people there's nothing there, you know, but there was something that I saw that was there all the time. My grandpa told me, "Don't go away. We might go away, but we'll come back. We'll help you. The powers of *Four Winds,* they'll be here. So be firm, be steadfast. You pray and don't feel sad. Don't feel emptiness. Don't feel loneliness." But when they left, I really felt bad.

There is an old story we have about that feeling after someone you love leaves this life. There was this puppy playing around in the woods, tall weeds, and grass near the camp. Then the camp crier comes, and he tells everybody to pack because the camp is moving. So everybody starts getting ready, but this little boy can't find his puppy. So everyone starts helping him look for that puppy, but it can't be found. So they leave the camp, and that little boy is looking back still crying for his puppy. And all the other kids are yelling and crying for that puppy, but they keep on moving.

So when I prayed, my grandpa and grandma were gone. I was like that little lost puppy. When I came back out of the woods to the camp it was dark, and I didn't know which way they went. So here I sat at the old campsite crying. It's empty, and it's lonely. [Black Elk continues the story about the lost puppy.] Then a scout came into the camp and called for this puppy. When the puppy saw this scout he was happy and started jumping around. So the scout picked up this puppy and took him, because he knew in what direction the people had gone. He traveled through the night on horseback, and at daybreak he caught up with the other people. So that scout brought that puppy home. That family and the kids were really happy. Nobody knew who that scout was. So it was a *two-legged* spirit that had brought that puppy back.

So when I pray now, my grandpa and grandma, everybody, is gone. The whole camp has moved out. This whole Western Hemisphere has moved out. So I'm just a little lost puppy sitting out in an old campsite, crying. Here some place I heard a horse, and I heard a voice. That scout came, and I recognized him and that horse. I was happy. So he comforted me and carried me back to my people.

Anyway, my grandparents had prayed to Tunkashila to bless me through this sacred Chanunpa, and the spirits gave me that power. They gave me at least one drop of wisdom and one drop of knowledge. I was given something that I could hold onto for our little ones and the unborn behind me. It was something they could rely on. It was something I could use to help lead them back to Tunkashila and Grandma. It was the power of the Four Winds, and it covered a huge distance. It was a good thing I didn't get educated in school; otherwise I would have lost this gift. I might have even gone against it.

So that happened to me when I was only five years old. I became an adult and learned about these sacred powers. From that age until I was nine, I caught all the terminology used in the universities today. In those four years everything was like a little moving picture. Everything that I see, hear, smell, taste—I have

a little color TV back there that records it. That's how I came to
know what I know. Everything I saw and everything I heard was
recorded in there, and I could rewind it and replay that little
picture. So there was always something new coming in. New
pictures were being recorded all the time. So I was given that
understanding that way. And in the spiritual power I could see
my people, my grandpa, my grandpa's father, and their fathers
and mothers, and it goes on and on. I could see the whole camp,
and I knew they were my relatives.

At the age of nine I held the sacred Chanunpa and went before Tunkashila and Grandmother. When darkness approached,
clouds started forming all the way around me, and there was
lightning underneath. Then the powers of the Four Winds came.
At first I experienced someone walking up behind me. I could
hear heavy footsteps coming—boom, boom, boom. With each
step the whole Earth trembled. The whole mountain started to
shake, and that gave me a spooky feeling. So I tried to shake it
off. "Okay, Black Elk, what's wrong with you? You come from
an intelligent, respectable family. Are you going to chicken out?"
I tried to give myself hell that way.

Pretty soon I heard a hooting in the distance. "Hooo. Hooo."
Like an owl, but it was real deep and real loud. So I knew they
were coming to me, and my heart started pounding. So that also
gave me a spooky feeling like somebody pouring cold water
down my back, and my ribs are sticking out, and water is trickling
down the ribs. At the same time I was trying to pray and trying
to listen to see what was going on. All three things were going
at once in my head, and my mind was running wild. It was kind
of funny how I observed all these things going through my head
at once, you know. I could hear my heart pounding loudly. So I
was standing there holding this Chanunpa and trying to give
myself hell and trying to give myself encouragement and trying
to listen and trying to pray all at the same time.

So I prayed, but I had to pray from my heart. All of my
concentration and thoughts went from my head to my heart. All
of my senses—hearing, smell, taste, and feeling—were connected
to my heart. So my spirit tried to understand the power that was
coming from behind me. "Hey, try to shake it off. Try to pray."

So I prayed, and now I was calm, but the footsteps were still coming. Another hoot again, and this time it's a little louder. As it gets closer, it gets louder. Then it was like my whole body became hollow, and that sound echoed up and down inside. It vibrated my whole body.

So I was standing there praying, and my mind was saying, "Gee, I must really be crazy. If I had a little sense, I should take off." But there was no sense in me, you know. As I was praying, I heard this hooting for the third time, and I heard that spirit say loud and clear, "I am coming. I am coming." It was like the hooting was on the outside, and his voice was on the inside. Then he hooted for a fourth time, and I felt a finger poking me in the top of my back, kind of pushing me. I almost flew off from there without wings! My head was going that way, but I stood firm and began to pray again. I was practically glued to the ground. So I was holding this Chanunpa and listening, and this voice said, "I am here. I am here." That's what he said. Again, "Hoo. Hoo," is what I heard on the outside, but his voice I heard on the inside.

Hey, I got company. I feel good now. Then that shadow of fear melted from me. It felt like someone comforting me by putting his hand on my head. Then he came around and stood in front of me and sat down. So I sat down. Now we could shoot the breeze. It really felt good! Then we conversed, and I could say anything I wanted. He answered all my prayers. He even revealed every word I had said, and he answered every word I said. (So when you go out there to pray, you'd better memorize what you are going to say. Sometimes words just come out of your mouth and go away.) Then he left. After he left there was a little stone lying there. So the stone people talk. So I learned a lot from that spirit.

So I learned about this sacred Chanunpa when I was nine years old. After I went back, one day I was holding this piece of wood and piece of stone [Sacred Pipe], and this little dog goes by. First time I saw him go by. So I said, "Hey, little guy, what's your name?" So he stopped and looked up. Then he answered me. All of a sudden I realized, "Hey, with this thing you could talk to this little guy here." So I was really excited. I was like a kid with a new toy. "Hey, with this Chanunpa you could talk to trees and talk to rocks and talk to buffaloes." I thought everybody knew about this little walkie-talkie. I thought everybody knew how to hear those little creatures. Also, I thought I was the last person to find this out, but soon I found out that nobody knew anything about it. So when I told people, they thought I was crazy or just talking through my hat. I was just a little guy, but my brain was big.

So my brothers and cousins were older than me. They'd go to school, and when they came back they'd call for me.

"Hey, little shrimp, come here. The teacher asked us these questions, and we don't know how to answer them. How shall we answer?"

Then I'd tell them. Then they would tell me to keep my mouth shut and go play with the kids my own age or go play with my bone horses. Then these big guys would go to school and tell their teacher the answers I had given them. When they brought their report cards home, they had straight As. But they never told who gave them those answers, and they told me to keep my mouth shut. So I would go crawl in and play with [children] my own age, but at the same time my head was real big.

So Tunkashila gave me those powers, and they also gave me a command. Instead of promoting and elevating me over everyone, they put me back to earth. They put me under the feet of everything that exists. Even that little ant has feet, and I'm underneath his feet. So I'm under the feet of all life. That's why my name is "Welcome." I'm just a little throw rug with *welcome* written on it. So you wipe your feet and go in the sacred arbor. That's how come people with sickness, worries, and sadness come to me. They wipe their feet and go on in to get to that good life. I was told to use this sacred Chanunpa as a cane and that would lead me to Tunkashila and Grandmother, where there is no end. It's everlasting life there.

So this Chanunpa is a cane. It has no end. So the old people, they called it a horse. It has a lot of strength and patience. The horse thinks real slow. But when he's finished thinking, his action is lightning fast. He does things lightning fast, but man is totally opposite. We think lightning fast, but we're real slow, real poky.

We're a lot slower than a turtle. So those old people tell really simple stories—like kid stories.

So I learned a lot from my grandpas and grandmas. Actually, in the Lakota way, I had eleven grandpas and grandmas that taught me these sacred ways. Sometimes they told stories, and sometimes they just said it real short. When it's short, you call them *sayings*. For example, they used to tell us that our days would be long for giving food to old people and little ones. So you should remember that. Always look for old people and orphans, because Tunkashila is then going to bless you for that. Your days will be long, and you're going to have wrinkles. Your buckskin is going to outlast all these modern materials. I wore out a lot of blue jeans, but I still wear my birthday suit.

So I could say that I was the first Indian boy that went all the way up through these powers. I went inside this communication [English language] to study the white man. It was like walking up to the Statue of Liberty. You go inside and walk up to her arms or go inside her head and look out through the crown. It was something like that. I went inside everywhere. I went into the heart. I went into the head and even looked out through his eyes to see what he sees, how he observes things. What I learned was that the white man, we call him *wasichu* [waa-she'-chew], has a real keen sense of eyes. They see values, so I give them credit for that. But what they don't see is the spirit.

I went into the ear, and I heard all this rock and roll music, radios, and televisions. When I went to the sense of smell, there were a lot of camouflages there. I smelled a lot of perfumes, but they were mostly based on alcohol. It didn't cure anything; it only camouflaged. So I saw that. Then the taste, there again everything was camouflaged. But what I saw there was mostly alcohol, like beer, wine, and whiskey. They like that taste, so they become alcoholics. It is a disease. You can't think straight, you can't walk straight, and it always drives you to madness. So they have to numb themselves, and they call it "relaxation."

Then I went to the feeling and the senses. All I saw were those little gadgets like temperature gauges that tell you how hot it is or cold it is. So they have all those little machines, because they don't know how hot or cold it is. So the whole structure was mechanized machines. So that's what I saw. Then I came back.

So you might say that I'm a scout for my people. It's tough to be a scout, really tough. To be a lone scout like me is even tougher, because you might run into a whole bunch of enemies. Then the odds would be against you, and you have to maneuver around to escape from many enemies. I'm not talking about just physical enemies. There are sicknesses and all kinds of death you have to maneuver around. But then there are the powers of the Four Winds. They come to your rescue. And when those buffaloes come, they stomp and tromp everything in their path. If cancer is in their way, they'll just tromp it to nothing. Anything— sadness, sorrow, sickness—they'll tromp it to nothing, to dirt. So they have those powers to destroy. Then they make things good again. They never bring anything bad. They only bring health and help.

So like this coyote, it has the same power. If troubled times come, you call on this little coyote, and he'll maneuver you out from the danger. He also has sacred powers. People use everything on him to get rid of him, like poisons, traps, guns, helicopters, and airplanes, but he still survives. So he has that power. So we have that power.

So I don't speak English, but I speak Lakota fluently, very fluently. If you understood Lakota, you'd be surprised, because I would tell you the answers to some of the mysteries your scientists are now probing. But when it comes to English, the funny part is I hear it loud and clear. I understand everything that is said. So I pray for you that you obtain the same power I have. You and I are no different. It's just that understanding. You just drifted away from it, just walked away from it for thousands and thousands of years. That's how come you have lost contact. So now you're trying to find your roots. They are still here. So I am able to communicate with you and help you that way. So I'm just a little tool, just a little instrument.

So I started with these powers when I was five years old, and now I'm sixty-eight. So that Ph.D. was built inside me. I was built with it. So I'm part of the *fire, rock, water,* and *green.* I am a product of Tunkashila's handwork, and Grandmother, she gave me birth. She gave me all these gifts free of charge. I never discovered anything. I never formed or shaped anything. [Black Elk refers to the use of the fire in metallurgy, chemistry, etc.] Maybe that's how come they call me a dumb Indian. I'm trying to trace down why they call me dumb. Maybe they're right, you know, or maybe I'm just having a mad dream. Then I pinch myself. "Hey, wake up." It's like that, so sometimes it's tough to be an Indian.

My people say that there were times it was tough to be a Lakota, or Earth Man. The way the spirit translated it, there is this immense body of water, and in the midst lay a long island. They call it *Turtle Island,* but in modern terminology it is known as "Western Hemisphere." The spirits told us that this is where peace lives. It is the home of peace, and *Lakota* means "peace." We're Lakotas. We're living legends. We're living evidence of peace. So there are times it's kind of hard to be a man of peace, but I'm still thankful to my grandfathers and grandmothers.

CHAPTER 2

Hard Times

I look like a scarecrow. Like I'm trying to scare something. I've dressed like this all my life—funny hat and funny shoes. That protects me. It's like a camouflage. The way I look serves me a purpose. I could go anywhere. I see a lot of people smile at me. It's not just out of love, but because I look funny. My sister-in-laws are always teasing me about it. They smile at me, and then someone says to me, "They didn't smile at you because you look good. You look funny, you know." They tease me that way. One time this teacher said to me, "You know, I want to tell you something, but I'm afraid you might get mad." So I said, "No, go ahead and fire. I won't get mad." So he said, "You know, you have the dumbest look on your face, but you're the smartest man I've ever known." That's what he said. Then I told him, "Oh, that's good. Thank you. That also protects me."

When I go someplace, most of the time those little people see me. At first they'll pretend not to see me. They go past me a little ways, and then they will turn back and look at me. Then they'll nudge their mama or daddy or grandma or grandpa, and I'll hear them say, "There's an Indian back there." So the Indians are still here. We never phased away. We didn't just blend into society and vanish. In fact, we're appearing more and more and more. We get around more now, too. Indians are not just confined only to the United States or one state or one county or one city or one house. They know us all over this Earth.

One time I was walking around in Washington, D.C. Of course, I dressed just like this—jeans, cowboy shirt, cowboy boots, big hat, and braids. All my pretty clothes are hanging in those museums. I didn't know they were so expensive. Their price tag is unbelievable! These here are ten cents or fifty cents or a dollar. I could pick up any of my clothes at the Salvation Army or just drive up to one of those boxes and grab myself an outfit and go on. They're cheaper, so I could wear them. I could discard them, pick up some more, like that.

Anyway, what happened to me in Washington, D.C., was that I was walking around, and nobody ever saw me. I was invisible. Nobody ever said hi to me. All these guys were wearing five-hundred-dollar suits, white shirts, and neckties. They were just whizzing this way and that way. So they didn't see me. It was really funny. Sometimes it's really funny to be an Earth Man. So I went inside that big dome, and there were people sitting there reading the newspaper. Out of the corner of my eyes I could see that they were watching over me. When I would look at them, they would look away and pretend they didn't see me. And there were people there taking pictures. Well, the object is over there, but at the last minute they would quickly turn their camera over here, snap it, and go on. But I knew what was going on. So we were kind of playing cat and mouse there.

Anyway, what really protects me is these things hanging over my ears [braids] and my complexion, these funny clothes, funny hat, and funny shoes. It camouflages me, so I could go anyplace, anywhere. All these materials that I wear, they are just substitutes. And maybe I look dumb on the outside, on top, but I'm not that way. That spiritual power I wear is much more beautiful and much greater. We call it *wisdom, knowledge, power, and gift* or love. There are these four parts to that spiritual power. So I wear those. When you wear that power it will beautify your mind and spirit. You become beautiful. Everything that Tunkashila creates is beautiful.

So my name is Wallace Howard, Wallace Howard Black Elk. And Wallace Howard is a cowboy. He's Scotch-Irish. He's a white man that was raised by my grandfather. So he knows the sacred ways and comes to the lodge, and the spirit comes in. He understands my people. So back in 1921, four days after I was born, he comes over with my uncle. They want that stuff he has, so they give him the honor to give me a name. So now he has to give me a name and a horse. He knows the Chanunpa. He knows these ways, but he wasn't prepared. So he got off from his horse and made me touch the rein of that horse. That was a signal that I accepted that horse and everything that was with it—bridle, martingale, saddle, thirty-thirty Winchester, saddlebags, lariat, silver mount, spurs, gloves, raincoat, and all that.

So he touched my little tiny hand to that rein to signal that I accepted all that stuff. Then he went on, "Now, I want to name you. I'm not prepared, so the only way I can do it is to give you my horse, my outfit, my name, and my language. So you're going to grow up to be a rough and tumble cowboy like me. You're going to be a bronco rider." So he was going on that way.

That was a cowboy prayer, see? But these are sacred ways, so that was also a real prayer. I'm alive. I'm not just a piece of rag. But that was his prayer, because that was the way he was. He didn't know how to say the Lord's Prayer or a bunch of Hail Marys, because he's a cowboy that was raised by my people. But he's an Irishman, so he has his own language and speaks English. He married one of my relatives. That's how come I have cousins that have blue eyes and blond hair. If I brought them here and told you this is my cousin, you wouldn't believe it.

Later that prayer becomes reality. Because he gave me his name, he taught me English and Irish, and I taught him Lakota. So he could communicate with my grandpa and grandma. I also became a bronco rider in the rodeos. But I lost a lot of that Irish language because nobody here speaks that language. So if I go back there [Ireland], I could speak Irish, too. Now you know where I got these funny shoes and hat, funny clothes. It was from that cowboy. So I pray for him, and a spirit comes in. He's a Scotch-Irish, so he speaks Irish in the Chanunpa ceremony.

So I carry that name Wallace Howard, but I grew up in the sacred ways of my people. I was trained that way. You have to have a lot of patience to follow that sacred path. I remember when it came time for my first Chanunpa. I kept asking my grandpa, kept bugging him, "How do you make Chanunpa?" Well, he just kept going about his business, and it seemed to me that he never heard me, but I kept asking. He just didn't answer me. He would just keep on working or keep on riding or say that it was time to go chop wood, but he would never answer my question. It seemed to me like he wasn't ever paying any attention when I asked him over and over. Finally, one day he said, "Grandchild, we're going to go over there, and you're going to hunt that Chanunpa stem."

So we went up this creek in our wagon. It was a dry creek bed. We were going to look for some ashwood, and he knew there was some along that creek. When we got to this one spot, he said there should be some ashwood up the bank and sent me off to look for it. So I went up there and found a cluster of ashwood. He told me just what size to look for, so I had to use my ingenuity to figure out which tree was the right tree. Also, it had to be perfectly straight. First, I prayed, and then I just sat there looking at that cluster of trees. Then I got up and started walking all the way around trying to select one. "Not that one; it has a little curve in it. Not that one; it has limbs coming out the side. Not that one; it also has too many limbs." I was going like that all the way around. Then I came back to where I started, so I sat down and started praying again. All of a sudden, I saw one right in front of me, right in the middle of that cluster.

So I went off in all four directions. First I went to the south, and I found a little opening through which I could see that tree. Okay, it looked straight. So I went on to the west side and looked towards the east. There was a little opening there, and I could see that tree. I went to the north, and there's an opening there also. "Okay, that's it!" So I went back and went east to west and prayed. I put a little mark on there, a little cloth. Then I went back down to the creek bed and told my grandpa I had found the right tree.

"I found the tree! I found it!" He believed me and said, "Yes, you're a good boy." So he measured the length of time it had taken me to find that tree. Maybe he had been watching me from someplace. I don't know. Anyway, I led him back to where I had prayed. He sat down, and I pointed it out. "See. It's right in the middle. Straight West." So he brought out the Chanunpa, filled it, and prayed. Then he sat there looking. Finally, he said, "I see it. I see it." Then he goes to the south and looks through that little opening to see that tree. Then he went to the west and looked at that tree and to the north and looked at that tree. "Good boy, you found it!" So he sights in on that tree, and we went there. He prayed and sprinkled tobacco all the way around the tree. Then he said, "So let's go home."

Now I thought we were going to measure it, hack it off, put it in the back of the wagon, and haul it home. That is what I thought. But we went back without it. On the way home he said, "We'll come back for it." So I wasn't really in gear in my mind to understand what he was saying. I didn't understand the meaning in his language. I didn't have enough patience to really hear what he was saying. So I thought, "Okay, maybe we'll come back tomorrow for it." Tomorrow comes, and we have to go someplace. "Okay, it might be the next day." Next day comes. It's stone-people-lodge day. So we have to go cut some wood for the ceremony. So it might be the third day. So my mind kept on running along like that, you know. But I'm just a kid, so I'm impatient. Every day I waited. Pretty soon one month had passed by. "Maybe he forgot. It might be next month." I kept on going on in my mind like that. I kept trying to figure it out. Pretty soon fall went by. Then winter passed and spring came.

All the green was out again, and grandpa said, "Grandchild. Hitch up those horses. We're going to go see that tree." By then I had waited a long time, and it had passed. If he had said that we were going over there next year, that would have been okay with me by that point. I had worried myself to death. Besides that, I thought by then that he had forgotten all about it. Then, just about the time I was getting ready to forget about it, he remembered. Now, he didn't say we're going to bring it back, just that we were going to go see it. But, again, I was off thinking that we were going to cut it, load it, and bring it back.

That evening was a long evening for me. I kept thinking that before long I'd have my own Chanunpa, first one. I had a lot of things going around in my head because of how I had been educated up to then. I still had two parts. I'm an Earth Man, and I'm still a little guy. So we went there, and all of the trees had green leaves sprouted out except that straight one we had picked out. We went to it, and grandfather began praying, "There will be a time that we are going to come here and take you with us." Right away my mind started up, "When? Next week? What day? What time? After church on Sunday?" My mind started running like that, but I tried to ward it off. By then I wanted to try to have a little patience.

So then it went on. The next year, that fall, that winter, and then the spring was coming around again. Grandpa said, "Let's go. Let's see." So we went back. We went to that tree, and he pulled off some bark and began to inspect it. There he saw those little guys [insects] making tunnels in there, so he said, "So, it's time." Then he notched the tree and pushed it down from north to south. Then we cut it to the right size. Next my grandpa takes a straw and begins to poke around in the center of the tree. It's filled with dry powder. So he began poking around in the powder and making a deep hole in there. Then he tears off the bark, picks up one of those little guys and pushes him into that hole he made. Right away that little creature starts digging in and pushing that powder out of the hole. Pretty soon he had worked clear through to the other end. Then grandfather thanked that little guy and put him back. "Thank you. Go back to your food. Go back to your shelter. Go back to your home." Like that. Then we prayed, left there, and brought that piece of ashwood home.

Right away I could already see myself whittling away, but grandpa had other plans. He told me to take it into the lodge. There he instructed me how to cross-stack up some wood and place that piece we had brought back in the middle. Then I had to stack three more pieces on top of that. Then he said we would leave it there for the rest of the summer and through the winter.

The following year we made a journey over to the stone quarry. That is over in Pipestone, Minnesota. That stone—you call it *catlinite*—is found only in that place. You can't find it anywhere else in the world. It is a red stone. Our old people say that it is the blood of the buffaloes that gave their life so that we could live. That blood turned to stone. It took us four days to get there by wagon. We brought along all our food and made camp four times before we got there. Then we worked for eight days and nights to remove it from the ground. We dug way down into the ground, removing the dirt a bucketful at a time. There were a lot of big boulders in there also. Finally, we broke through the granite, keep digging, removed that shell, and there it was. So we had found it. Then we pried it off and brought it back.

When we got home, grandpa laid out that stone and cut it into little elbows. Then we took the main one and began to drill out the bowl. We used willows, buffalo grease, and ashes. It took a long time to make that hole, so you have to have a lot of patience for that. Then we drilled out the hole in the stem. You have to make sure that stem hole aligns with that bowl. When that was finished, we had to shape the outside of the stone. Then we had to polish it. That also takes a long time. You use grease and ashes and rub it with a buckskin. So it took us a year before we were finished with that stone. Then we had to shape that stem to fit that stone. All in all, it took me four years to complete that Chanunpa. It took me four years, because I kept bugging him, "How do you make a Chanunpa?" I kept bugging him that way. I wish I hadn't asked all those questions. It was tough, you know. I didn't know what I had gotten myself into, but now I realize.

The knowledge [of Grandmother the Earth] is there all the time, but all those flimsy-whimsy ideas kept bugging me. My brothers, sisters, aunts, and uncles—they all went to school. So they yak, yak, yak. That's never ending. So, back from 1890 to the 1920s, they were going to school to the first, second, and third grades. One of my uncles went through to the sixth grade, six years. By then he's twenty-one, so he quit school. Now he's educated. Some of the others started when they were fifteen or sixteen, and only went for two years, because when you're eighteen you don't have to go to school anymore. So they only went to the second or third grade. There's no high school there, only school to the sixth grade. Anybody who goes there, we consider them educated. When they come back, they speak English, so their way of life is different then. Then this other way of life is totally savage for them. We're just ignorant pagans. They look at us that way.

When I was little, I would sit there watching my grandpa smoke his Chanunpa. Through that telepathic wave of intelligence, he would visit with the other old people. It's a silent communication. They know how to talk that way. Then my educated aunts and uncles would come over to visit the old people. They'd come there and just sit to listen to what they were talking about. But, because they were educated, they'd sit there and yak. But when they sat around the old people, there were no words coming out of them.

So they'd sit there for five or ten minutes, and no words were spoken. Because they were educated, they got impatient. "Hey, you two, you're sitting there like wooden Indians. You're sitting there like dummies. How come you don't speak to each other?" They talked to them like that, but they were visiting each other. They were talking, but these others came there and disturbed them.

So from that point of education the destruction begins. We are kind of losing that silent communication. When they use that English, it's full of *if*s, *but*s, *maybe*s, and words like that. Those words weaken your mind. That leads people later to say things like, "Well, to my recollection, I don't remember," or, "I don't recall," or, "Maybe I said that." They talk that way. Then you show them a piece of paper where they wrote it down. "Oh, yes, I said it, but I didn't really mean it." So that's the educated way to talk. You could whip two tongues at the same time in there. So you could always change your mind. That's why my old people told me that English was a dangerous language.

But with this Chanunpa way, you are going to whip just one tongue. You're going to have only one mind, one heart, and one spirit. You have to hold that Chanunpa straight. We often talk about holding the Chanunpa straight. So I learned from making my first Chanunpa that I don't want to be asking my grandpa questions all the time. What I learned was to listen to him real carefully. I really got myself into it, and there's no way of backing out now. I'm in it now. I have to stay with this way.

So my grandpa taught me a lot. For instance, how to respect and how to have a little patience. So I was out there with those old people and old ways. I lived and grew up right there. I grew up with the power of the Chanunpa. So that is built right into me. We don't go to K-Mart and buy a Chanunpa, then crawl into the lodge, and the *medicine* comes out. It's not that way. It's not like *hogie-pogie* where you pull a rabbit, a bunch of flowers, or some silk cloths out of a hat. A lot of people expect that, but it's not that way. It's a way of life. It's a path. This Chanunpa is not a chalice. It's not a wine; it's not a bread, not like that. It's not a religion. You live with it. You take care of it. You bundle it away. So there is no "Sacred Pipe religion."

Also, we have a main Chanunpa. Just one, it's the main one. It is never exposed to the public or someone who just walks in. People have to understand that Chanunpa. For instance, a lot of women will come in on their moon time [menstrual period] and contaminate the Chanunpa. Those people have to learn to respect themselves and this Chanunpa. Even a man—his clothing might be contaminated from being near a woman on her moon. So you have to purify yourself with sage. You have to wipe yourself clean. So the spirit told us, "When your robe [body] is soiled or dirty, don't come near the Chanunpa. Never let any man with dirty hands touch that Chanunpa." That's what he said. Even if we wash, take a shower, scrub ourselves with soap, and then put on those aftershaves, body lotions, and deodorants, that won't camouflage that contamination. When you are dirty, you have dirty thoughts. So you have to come to that Chanunpa with a clean mind. That's what the spirit meant.

So what we are talking about here is sacred. One little part of you is sacred. So there are a lot of things you have to understand, not just this Chanunpa. But when you start to study that Chanunpa, it connects up everything. It connects all life. So my instructions are to try to understand this Chanunpa in a really simple way, because that's the way I started. I started when I was only five years old. So if a dumb Indian who's only five years old can understand this Chanunpa, I think there are a lot of people out there who could have a better understanding of it. If they have that higher education, they should have a higher understanding. They should have a better brain. I don't have that degree. I don't have that piece of paper, so that puts me lower than them.

So it's better for me to be an Earth Man. I can see everything from the outside. Looking inside the culture of the white man, I can see and understand everything. Lucky for me I didn't go in there, or they would have torn me apart. In some mysterious way, my grandfather and grandmother asked those sacred powers to give me a power so that I could continue in our old ways. So they hung onto me and gave me this power. But back in the 1920s and 1930s, those were the hardest times I ever went through.

They used to preach against us in the twenties and thirties. That was the peak. There were no moccasins. There were no buffaloes to chase. The government set up schools and forced us to go. They cut our hair and changed our clothes. They forced us to speak English, and that caused us to lose our culture—language, customs, and ways. If you spoke Lakota, they would wash your mouth out with yellow laundry soap. You'd have to repeat in English what the teacher said. If you had to repeat it twice, you'd get a reward. They would put a clothespin in your ear. If you couldn't repeat it a second time, then another clothespin would be added. So I usually had about six clothespins in my ear. Or they would make you hold out your hand, and then the teacher would hit it with a ruler ten times to remind you of the Ten Commandments. Sometimes they would break that ruler.

Other times I would have to stand on my tiptoes. I would have to stand real still. Sometimes I might have to stand there forty-five minutes or fifty minutes. If I fell, they would whip me. So I had to stand there real stiff. I had to endure that. It took a lot of courage and endurance just to stand there and balance yourself for ten minutes. At your desk you would have to sit there with both feet together, your eyes forward, your pencil at a forty-five-degree angle pointing to your shoulder, your lips together, and all that. Then you would have to push your pencil with your elbow and have good penmanship all in the name of a forty-five-degree angle. Anyway, there were terrible things going on then. But now over here we have doctors, and they have the poorest handwriting. You can't even read their writing for prescriptions. So it's really something. We had really hard times.

Those Christian people would preach against everything we did. They'd say, "Don't go out there and eat those roots and herbs. Those are serpent food, devil's food. We have a hospital, so you come over here and eat those registered pills." So we were supposed to go over there and eat the right kind of poison. So we'd go over there, and they would have that St. Joseph's aspirin. At the same time, over here Jesus is the healer. So what's wrong with Jesus? Why do I have to eat those pills from St. Joseph? So all this was going through my head. So I had a heck of a time trying to understand.

I didn't want to go to school, so I would hide out with my grandpa and grandma. I refused to go there. Then they would track down my grandpa and grandma and take me back. Sometimes they even threw us in jail for it. The longest time we stayed in jail was for ten day—ten days with bread and water. I had committed a crime because we chose to worship Tunkashila. So it was for no reason at all. So we were in prison many times, not just one time, but many.

The really tough part was that it was our own people who were tracking us down. They were Indian people. They wore uniforms and badges and carried clubs and guns. There were no roads, so they would ride over there on horseback. When they came they would tear up our sacred stone-people-lodge—break it up and throw it in the fire. If they found one of our *sacred bundles,* they'd tear that up and throw it into the fire. If they found a Chanunpa, they would just smash that stone into a million pieces and throw the stem into the fire.

So we would have to sneak out to the mountains to perform our ceremonies. We would ride way out there on horseback. We had to carry everything with us: blankets, buckets, our Chanunpa, our sacred bundle, or whatever we could carry. We'd send a scout on ahead, and he would be standing on the mountaintop and signal us if the coast was clear. So we would ride over there near the spot and then let our horses go, and from there we went on foot. But they were always trying to catch us. They knew where the waterhole for the horses was, so they'd go there and hide. They'd wait there until somebody came along, and then they would grab them and try to make them tell where we were holding our Chanunpa ceremony.

So when we went there we had to hurry. We had to do everything real fast like. We could build a lodge in no time, or we would poke a hole in the side of the mountain so we could go in there and have a Chanunpa ceremony. We would have to heat up the rocks real fast and use just the right kind of wood so there would be no smoke they could see, just flame. We knew all that. We would make our tobacco ties, fill the Chanunpa, heat up the rocks, hurry. Then we would go in, and the medicine, the spirit, would come in. Pray. Hurry. Finish. Then we would hide our *robes* [sacred flags used in the ceremony] and pick everything up, disassemble the lodge, put the wood back in the woods, put our rocks all over or cover them up, cover up the damage, like that. Then we would take off and scatter in all directions. Sometimes I would come back on foot. So we had to go through all that. So that was kind of hard and sad.

But I was equipped, nineteen generations ago I was equipped to plow right on through. Sometimes those soldiers [Indian police] got hurt shortly thereafter. One time they came over there and tore everything up. On the way back home, this guy's horse spooked, and it threw him. But his foot got caught in that stirrup, and he was dragged to death. So they had sickness come to them and accidents. One guy's wagon overturned on him, and another guy's house burned down, and he lost his children in the fire. In some of those families, the whole family died. So those things happened. So we kept going.

Then those black robes, like Father Fagan, they would give us a rough time also. If we didn't go to church four times a month, they would hold back our food rations. So if we missed church, just once or twice, there would be no commodities issued to us, and we would starve. So we would have to wait until the next month and make those four churches. Then they would give that food to us. So they used that food to expand their membership or to prevent us from worshiping Tunkashila and having our Chanunpa ceremonies and lodges.

Then, like, Father Fagan, he would sneak up on us. He would come into the camp and go from village to village. He would go around asking everybody, "Did you hear any drumming?" He knew we used that noisemaker in our ceremonies, so he was trying to figure out if we were still doing that pagan stuff, see? Then somebody might accidently say, "Well, I heard a drum over there." Then he'd write the name of that person down, but he wouldn't stop there. He'd write everybody's name down in that family. He'd write down the names of the old people there and even that little baby's name. But that baby can't even talk. So he'd go through four or five families like that and make a long list of all those names. He'd have maybe a hundred names written down on that list. Then he would go over to the [reservation] superintendent, and he'd say, "I've got a list here of one hundred people who are complaining about those people having a sweat-lodge. They are making all this unnecessary noise, beating on the drum and keeping them awake. So they are complaining." Well, that's not what those people said, but he wrote it down that way. They didn't intend it that way, but that's what he told the superintendent. So the superintendent, he doesn't check those names—those names of little kids and babies—he just says, "Okay, chief, how many soldiers you got?" "Well, I got eight lying around here." "Okay, get them on horseback and go over there. If you find a sweat-lodge or anything, just tear it up." So that's the government people. They did that against us. They would pit Indian against Indian. So that came back on us and made it hard for us.

So I went through those things, and it was hard and sad. My people were always getting hurt. But through the Chanunpa, through some mysterious power, we were always in good health and good spirit, because when that spirit comes in you ask for help and health. During these hard times the spirit kept encouraging me, "Keep going. Keep going. I'm here. Nothing is going to happen to you. I'm going to help you. Tunkashila is going to help you. I want to send help to you." Like that. So, at the end of World War II when I came back, there was Father Fallon. "Don't go to *yuwipi* [a Lakota spirit ceremony]. Don't go to the Chanunpa ceremonies. Don't talk to the devil. Don't let those demons possess you. Don't eat those medicines, because that's snake food they give you." He used to preach to us that way. Then there is powwow. Powwow is mortal sin. Bingo is mortal sin. Gambling is mortal sin. But when I came back, there was all this banging and noise going on over there. So I asked this guy, "Are they repairing that meeting house?" He told me there was going to be a dance in there, and I said, "No fooling!" So he tells me that Father Fallon is now the superior, and he loves dancing.

So we went in, and here is Father Fallon. He had his robe tied up in back, and he was leading the dancing. It was an Indian dance with feathers and everything. I was still wearing my army uniform, and he saw me right away. He came straight over to me and said, "Hey, Black Elk, let's go outside and talk." So we went outside. Then he tells me that while I was away at war they got new, high holy orders. The holy father had changed those laws for the reservations. Now we could have powwows. Also, now we could dance—not too much, just a little bit. If we danced too much, that would be black. It would be a mortal sin. So we could dance a little bit but not too much. So little bit by little bit we were beginning to crack that shell.

So when I came back from the war we had a ceremony, a lodge. Somebody came and tapped on the door. My grandpa, my dad, my cousins, my uncle, they said, "Now you've got a visitor." They wanted to know how well I was going to handle this visitor, because now I've grown up and I'm running the ceremony. I'm the one who is sitting by the door and pouring the water. I'm the one who filled the Chanunpa and has that power. So they wanted to see how well I was trained, how well I'm going to handle this visitor. So I said, "Tunkashila, we filled the Chanunpa, and now we're only here for health and help. So please do come in."

So we sang a song, and that visitor came into the lodge. Then something cold and slippery hit me on the chest and hit my grandfather on the forehead. It kept going around and around in the lodge. It hit me on the leg and then on the back and kept on going in a circle. You could hear water gurgling in there, and each time it hit, you felt something cold and slippery. That slap would make a sound, like "queeek, queeek." Then Grandpa said, "Someone came in and went that way. It came around and went back to where you are sitting. Do you know what it is?" So I said, "I forgot to ask him." That made them all laugh.

So everybody heard that water gurgling. It was amazing, because that sound was coming from those hot rocks. So it was water flowing through those hot rocks, and it was the *fish people* that had come in. They just swam right into that lodge. Then I heard them say in Lakota, "We are *fish-people*. We came from the bottom of the ocean to visit you. We came here to tell you that these people on the top [of the land], they are using that wisdom, knowledge, power, and gift from the Creator to take that sacred fire and pack it into a destructive tool [A-bomb]. What is happening is that they are dropping the residue from that into the water, and it's going to affect us fish-people. That radiation is going to go up to the surface and is going to float across the land. It's going to harm all the green, and it's going to harm the *winged, four-legged, creeping-crawler* creatures, mammals, and it's going to affect you *two-legged* creatures. So that is the reason why we came here, to tell you this."

So the nuclear residues were being secretly dumped into the ocean at that time. And nobody knows nothing about it, see? So when I began to tell people what I had learned in that lodge, they thought I was crazy. They told me not to tell the scientists or congressmen or religious leaders what the fish-people had said. They said that if I ever made such a statement in public, I would be questioned about it, and if I couldn't prove it, that I probably would be thrown in the slammer. But what I learned from those fish-people then, the world found out about seventeen years later. Seventeen years later we found out that the ocean was being used as a dump for nuclear waste, and only then we put a stop to it. But by then it was already affecting all the green underneath the water and those fish-people. The whales were coming to shore and dying, and people were eating contaminated fish. So for years it was lie on top of lie in the name of science. But through this sacred Chanunpa, we know what's going on all the time.

So that happened to me just after World War II. So now here a few years later Father Fagan got sick. He went to many hospitals, but they couldn't cure him. So we told him that he should come to the lodge and that we would pray for him. So he said, "Okay, I think I'll do that." Here he had been preaching against us all this time, but now he was really sick, and no one else could help him. So he came to the lodge, and that spirit came in and touched him and removed that pain. So he said, "Well, that's good. As long as they are not hurting me, I think that's all right." Pretty soon others came. So we overpowered that negativity. We reestablished our ways. In fact, later I even trained a Catholic priest, and he contacted the spirit through this sacred Chanunpa. It took him nine years to do that. In turn, he went to the Catholic congress and told those guys that the Chanunpa was really true and that they should stop trying to convert the Indians to Christianity. He actually said that. So at least he said something good for my people.

Over the years now things have changed on my reservation. They used to talk about me behind my back. They would tell everyone that I was a devil worshiper. They said I was possessed by demons. They all made those kinds of remarks. But now, just in the past few years, when I go back, everybody comes up to me and shakes my hand. They tell me they have been to a lodge or they had a Chanunpa ceremony and prayed for someone. So now I hear them saying "our Chanunpa" and "our sweat-lodge" and that kind of thing. So we plowed right through those hard times with the power of this sacred Chanunpa.

CHAPTER 3

The Earth People Philosophy

It takes a lot of courage to talk about these powers. It takes a lot of courage to be a witness. Back in 1905 and 1908 some commissioners came from Washington, D.C., to investigate the Chanunpa. They wanted to know if it was true or not—whether it was witchcraft or really from God. They had those kinds of thoughts. So we do have a little piece of paper somewhere about that visit. Then they wrote laws about our using these powers. For instance, Congress wrote a law that it was illegal for us to practice soul-keeping. So they wrote it that way. "Release all those spirits. That's an order. That's a law."

But whether there's a law or no law, we could still go out there. We don't need a piece of paper to contact those spirits. We go out there and crawl in the stone-people-lodge. Then we send a voice to the Creator—"Yo-ho"—and somebody responds and comes in. Even if somebody drags me out there with no Chanunpa or anything, I could still say, "Yo-ho. I'm lost. I need help." Then a spirit comes there and takes me some place. They'll fly you there. They'll take you any place. If you want to visit the moon, they'll take you up there. If you want to visit the star-people, they'll take you up there. They'll put you in one of those little flying saucers, and they'll zoom you up there in no time. Then, they'll bring you back.

They say that at one time we were civilized and educated. My grandfather told me that. They say we could talk to the trees and all the green. They say we could talk to the winged-people, the four-legged, creeping-crawlers, mammals, and fish-people. They say that at one time we could all talk to each other. No matter how many countless languages, forms and shapes, and symbols there were, they say we all spoke the same mind. That is called civilized, or educated. Well, we kind of drifted away from there and drifted over here. Now we call ourselves the civilized, Christianized world, but we just formed a little world all of our own. Then we got ourselves caught over here without spirit, and we ended up with zero.

But some people still have those powers. Some people just toy around with those powers, but they have no power to cure cancer, polio, tuberculosis, or anything. They just demonstrate a power. You know, like lifting a ball from the earth, then releasing it from their hands, and it goes down part way. It stops midway or goes back up into their hands. We know and understand those powers, but to us they are sacred. You don't take part of those powers and use it for hogie-pogie. A lot of people expect that from us, but we don't use those powers that way.

We have a spirit that comes in and displays those powers. They'll do it in a good way to heal and let you know that you are a part of the spirit. They help us in many ways. We have one ceremony we perform to have those spirits help us find special rocks that have sacred paints in them. We have to go to the Badlands to get that powdered paint. Layers of rainbow colors lie there. Those colors are inside the rocks that lie there. They are little lumps. On the outside they are grey, but when we take them home and crack them open, that paint is there on the inside. It's like a little compact.

So we go there and pray. We go there in the night when there is no moon. Then the spirit comes in and directs us where to go to find them. Then we take our Chanunpa and go over there in the pitch dark to look for those rocks. Then we pray, and you can see those special rocks glow in the dark. They look like little colored lights in the dark. You can see the colors that are on the inside. So we go there and take the colors that we need.

There were some young guys that heard we went there to pick

those rocks. They were educated. So when they heard about this, they ran down there with their little pick hammers. They started breaking up all those rocks to find those paints. They were all over the mountain breaking rocks. But they didn't find any, because they didn't go there with that spiritual knowledge. So those rocks hid. They just left. Those guys just saw those rocks with their naked eye, but they didn't see the colors. When you have the spiritual knowledge, those colors sing. So the spirit will educate you that way. You don't go there and just pick out your favorite color. It's not that way. You don't say, "That's the only one I love," or, "I don't favor the other colors." You don't talk like that. You can't just separate them and pick your one favorite color. So the spirit will come and educate you how to use those colors. I think the spirit uses colors in many different ways.

Anyway, I learned from the spirit how to find those rocks that contain the sacred powdered paints. I learned their songs, but there are many songs out there. There are countless songs. Like the fire, it has a song. That fire shapes and forms all life, and each shape has a song. And the rocks, the rocks have songs. Like this rock I wear around my neck, it has a song. All the stones that are around here, each one has a language of its own. Even the Earth has a song. We call it Mother Earth. We call her Grandmother, and she has a song. Then the water, it has a song. The water makes beautiful sounds. The water carries the universal sounds. Now the green. This tree, every green has a song. They have a language of their own. There's a life there. You say there is a chemistry language there. So each green has a song. There's a lot of songs we don't know yet. One man could never get to know all of them.

If you see a tree, it doesn't move. It doesn't talk or walk. You just see it. You just see a tree. That's all. But the trees talk. They have a language of their own. So all this green that you see, they communicate. There's a scent produced. I think over here you call it air or oxygen. So there is a communication going on, see? So each one of these green gives out a particular odor or scent. Then a little creature comes here and eats. There are many beautiful butterflies, but one of them eats this particular green. Then one of the winged creatures comes and eats the butterfly, but there's a poison inside. So he will detect that particular odor, because the butterfly also has a scent. The scent, the communication, it talks. So when they see that nice breakfast sitting there they detect that scent, so they don't eat it. But some go put it in their mouth. Then, "Oh, I tasted that one, and it really tastes awful." So the next time they see that color it's a warning. So there is a communication. Some are edible, and some transfer the power from one to another. So one could survive from the other, see?

So each one of the winged-people has a song. It is the same with the four-legged and creeping-crawler creatures. So that's how come we have an eagle song, a buffalo song, and even a serpent song, a serpent language. And it is there for those mammals and fish-people also. So recently the scientists discovered that the whale also sings. They listened to see if they had a language, and they had a sing-song. So every creature has a song. Every two-legged spirit and each one of the *Thunder-Beings* has a song. Even that spider, we call him *iktomi,* he walks, he rolls, he flies, and he sings a song. So we have medicine songs for that spider, *iktomi* songs. So I want to tell you that you have a lot to learn. What you know today, it's just a little bit—like the blink of an eye. So that power is immense.

We used to use those powdered paints to make our prayer ties. We call them tobacco ties or prayer ties. We would take a little piece of hide and place a pinch of tobacco in it. Then we would bring the outer edges together and tie it off into a little bundle. Each bundle was a prayer. Then we would paint each of those tobacco ties the colors the spirit had instructed us to use. Today our prayer ties are different. We don't use hides or those powdered paints any more. Instead we use small squares of colored cloth. The cloth has to be 100 percent cotton. So it's a substitute. We started using substitutes back four or five generations ago. So most of my people come from three generations ago, and they use those little substitutes. My grandfather was the first one to use those colored cloths. The spirit told him to use that substitute, because the buffaloes were gone.

So if you go to the Rosebud [Indian] Reservation [in South Dakota] today, you'll find eight thousand of us that look like me. But there are only forty-seven families that are real, are traditional. The others look like Indians, and they call themselves Indians, too. They are proud of that. If you ask them what they are, they'll say, "I'm Sioux," or like that. They talk about these powers like they knew all about them, but they never went to a stone-people-lodge. They never went to a *vision quest*, and they never went to a Chanunpa ceremony. In fact, they really don't believe about these powers, because they are Christians. So they denounced their own language, and they think these powers are devil's work. They talk like that. So you are going to find that some of the people look like me, but that they are educated and really don't believe in these powers. But we are the Earth People. We are steadfast and honest. We are true to our commitment, and we stay right in there. So the spirit comes to us.

So with me it's entirely different. Grandmother, she gave us this fire, and she gave us this rock, and she gave us this water, the rivers, lakes, and oceans, and she gave us all the green. She gave us a birth and a life. She put enough food here on this table [land], and she even put food inside the water. So those people that live in the water, they own that water. So they have the right to live there and eat the green. They breathe also.

And so on this long island [North and South America] she put all the food here. So we could sit here and eat. Our buffaloes could eat grass, so they could go anywhere. And we could go anywhere—park or hitchhike or pack a backpack. So we could go any place, and we didn't need a permit. You could sit down and enjoy this creation. When this Earth Man goes to a bubbling brook, he just sits there and drinks and admires. He listens to that wind whistling through the green and talks about the beautiful sounds made by the winged-people and all of life. That is the philosophy of the Earth People. But if a scientist goes to that same place, the first thing he will think of is how to make that "damn" water work for him. He'll want to put a dam there and a high-turbine generator. But the Earth Man will just sit there and listen to that bubbling brook and the wind. So that is our philosophy.

The base of the knowledge is the *fire, rock, water, and green.* But when that power was given to man, he used it to twist his own mind. Tunkashila gave man just one drop of that wisdom. But when you look up and see the power of Tunkashila, it's huge. It's immense. He wears a blue robe, and it's a huge robe. In the center of the heart of Tunkashila is that sun sitting up there. It's sacred. It's holy. We know he's the director of the universe of universes, and everything is a circle. So we know that everything was a circle from the beginning. The spirits took my grandfather to that sun. He told me that the sun has four holes in it, and that there is a land inside. We also know that the power was placed here for man, but man twisted his mind and took that [fire/nuclear] power into his own hands. That was like a naughty kid, so Tunkashila is going to spank him for that.

So man was given one drop of wisdom, one drop of knowledge, one drop of power, and one drop of gift or love (or talent). Tunkashila is the wisdom in itself. The knowledge is a woman, and we call it the Earth. We call it fire, rock, water, and green. So the basis of the knowledge is the fire. In our language we speak of the *peta wicoicage*—the "fire generation." All the shapes and forms of life originate from the fire. In your scientific language you call it the atom. The rock we call *maka*. *Maka* is the Earth. So we have *Grandfather* who is the wisdom and Grandmother who is the knowledge. But the wisdom and knowledge are really one.

So in the Earth People philosophy you have to understand this fire, rock, water, and green. For instance, the radioactivity is a part of the fire. So when man twisted his mind and took that fire, later he realized that he didn't know how to neutralize the radioactivity. The scientists still don't know how to neutralize the radioactivity. We Earth People do have a medicine that will neutralize it. But if we aren't careful with it, we could neutralize everything. Then all life would be destroyed.

So I have to learn, too. So I go back to the Earth People philosophy. I go there where there is the wisdom, power, knowledge, and gift. The fire, rock, water, and green are there, and all life is there, see? So when I'm there I really feel happy! I'm closer. But if I'm dragging around over here [in Western culture], it's really scary. When I come into this jungle, it's really scary. Somebody over here is watching every move I make. They are watching me to see if the spirits tell me something they don't want me to know. So I'm being watched. I know it, and I sense it. In between, I have to starve; I have to go without food and water in order to communicate with Tunkashila. So for doing that, the spirits gave me additional power so I could go in further and advance and lead my people. So this spirit came a few days ago and told us that more people will come to the Chanunpa now, because they sense and know that the world destruction is coming real fast now. So there will be a lot of tears.

When we Earth People call the medicine man, he comes in. So like the spirits say, "Anyone who prays to me with tears, I will listen. I will go there and help. I'll do anything he asks me. I will do it." So then he comes and reconstructs the human mind or reconstructs the human organs where the *toka* [enemy] has done damage. Also, that medicine man is not racist. After all, he's the Creator. He created and formed all life. So he can't denounce his own creation. So he doesn't come in and say, "I'm a Commanche spirit," or, "I'm an Apache spirit," or, "I'm only going to come in just for Lakota." He never comes that way, but even some of my Lakota people think it's that way. But I don't have that [attitude] inside me when I go to that power. There's no time for that. I go there with a clear, conscious mind. So the spirit comes in for anyone who prays in a humble way. He comes over, "Oh, poor little doggy." He'll pet you. He comforts and consoles you. Then whatever you prayed for, he'll answer that prayer. So that is science, see? That is the real science!

So I was the first one to be hand-picked and trained in these powers by my grandfathers and grandmothers. My grandfather used to warn me, "Now you are getting to that point. So don't be asking for mink coats, diamonds, and things like that. It's not that way." So my grandfather was really smart. Really smart! He never went to school, yet he understood everything. So we have a chance to use this power to overcome the evil in the world. So where does the evil get its power? The evil in itself has no power. So where does it come from? It comes from us. It crawls and creeps into our brains. We twist our own minds. We take that sacred knowledge and use it to fashion a gun. Then we call that knowledge power. So there is all this traffic between our ears, and that is where the evil comes from.

Grandmother the Earth is asleep. At the same time she knows—she smells, tastes, feels, sees, and hears everything. The whole world is her eyes. The whole world is her ears, sense of smell, taste, and feeling. But at this time she's asleep. So we Earth People have to poke a little hole [build a stone-people-lodge] in the Earth so she could breathe and communicate with us. Then we put the fire [hot rocks] back in there. Put those stone-people in there. Then we offer a little green [burn cedar on the hot stones], and we offer a little water [pour water on the hot stones]. We always remember Tunkashila first. We always honor Tunkashila the Creator, because Grandmother and Tunkashila are one.

So I learned from the old people that those spirits that come are my relatives. They learned that from the spirit. The spirit told them, "This Chanunpa is your relative. The powers of the Four Winds are your relatives. Pray to them. Talk to them. They are your relatives. To the West, the Thunder-Beings, they are your relatives. Send a voice out there. These are your relatives. Look that way. These are your relatives. Look to the North, the Buffalo Nation, the *White Buffalo-Calf Maiden,* the Chanunpa, these are your relatives. To the East, the Elk Nation, Black Elk, and the Elk Nation Woman that brings joy and happiness, these are your relatives. To the South, the Swan, the two-legged spirits that bring joy and happiness, the medicine people that bring health come from there. These are your relatives. Above you is the *Eagle Nation.* They watch, control, govern. They control the weather. They are the true meteorologists. These are your relatives. Down to the Earth, the stone-people are your relatives. So when you go back, tell your people that these are all your relatives." That's what the voice said.

The old people say that we used to have that balance. Like we say we want to walk in balance. We want to live in harmony. We want our Mother Earth to heal. But these creatures, like the bird-people and the four-legged, they still have that balance. It's like a carpenter's level. You tilt it, and the bubble goes this way or that way to balance it. To balance it, you have to get that bubble right in the middle. It's the same with that magnetic balance in the brain, but man lost it. If it tilts this way, the bird has sense enough to go this way. If it tilts the other way, they bounce back. That's how come they go back and forth [migrate]. But man lost it. Man lost his navigation in this world. So he ended up not knowing which way was top or bottom or sideways.

These medicine people that come in are not just aspirin. They are spirits. They are plants. The enemy comes in and deteriorates some part of the human structure like the mind, heart, lung, bone, or blood. When you pray, whatever the enemy deteriorated, that is where the medicine goes to recreate and reform the human structure. In the Earth People philosophy our body is made up of four basic substances represented by water, corn, berries, and meat. This instruction was first brought to us by Elk Woman nineteen generations ago. She carries a drum and song that goes with it. So in our ceremonies you'll often see four wooden bowls there [on the altar] containing the *sacred food*—the water, corn, berries, and meat.

Take, for example, the buffalo. He gave his life so we could wear his robe. We wear buckskins and moccasins. We use his sinews for thread and his bones for needles. He is a vegetarian and eats grass. But the same elements that are in that grass are also in our body. So the buffalo eats grass and turns it into flesh and blood. We digest his flesh and blood. In turn, we get strength from this four-legged. We also use his robe for our tipi.

That tipi also has a deep meaning for us. Those tipi poles are nations. They are people. They are the *Tree of Life*. There will be a time that the strength of all nations will be tied together to form the tipi. Then those little pegs that we use to tie the buffalo robes together in the front of the tipi are like little children. We also pierce our skin during the Sun Dance. We put those pegs into ourselves to say thank you to Tunkashila, the Creator. We spill one drop of blood and one drop of pain in return to Tunkashila and Grandmother. It is the woman who gives birth to us all through pain and blood. So we return that with one drop of blood and one drop of pain.

So we all come from woman. Our Chanunpa consists of a stone and a stem. That stone is the female, the woman. Her blood ran into the ground and formed that red stone. That stem is male. It is also the Tree of Life. When the two are connected it produces the generation of life. At one time the Tree of Life towered here, but then it withered and fell over. However, my grandfather [Nick Black Elk] saw in his vision that the Tree of Life would come to bloom again. He saw that one tiny root of that tree was still alive. But over here in this other philosophy there is only the *Tree of Knowledge.*

So I was explaining how this medicine man works. This little guy goes inside and investigates everything. He sees everything. So the enemy does damage to the brain or heart or liver or kidney or whatever. He goes there. He sees, like X ray. He sees it, and he goes there and repairs whatever is damaged. He recreates all the molecules, genes, organics, fibers, or whatever the enemy damages. He recreates and reforms it. That is why he has his name. That is why we call him Creator. So he reconstructs the human mind and physical body. He recreates the human spirit, so that the spirit could wear its robe and walk with a clear mind. So that is just one medicine man at work.

When that spirit comes in, he never comes in and says, "Office call. Ten dollars please," or, "Service call. Twenty dollars please," and like that. "What's your social security number?" "Do you have any Medicare or Medicaid?" He never questions us like that. He just comes in and comforts and heals. Then he leaves. So that is our medicine man.

So it's good that you hear about this medicine we have. I'm not a medicine man. Many people think that way, but that's not the way it is. The medicine is out there. Like I wear medicine. He's around here somewhere. So I say, "I need your help, my friend. I need your help." Then I fill the Chanunpa. "Hey, where are you?"

Then he comes in, "I'm right here. What do you need?"

So I tell him, "Well, this guy here needs your help." That way he gets help. The medicine man brings the help. Sometimes they bring health. So the two key words the Chanunpa carries are *help* and *health.*

Now the drugs. There are many drugs. They're countless. My people, my family, we held 311 different medicines. After the white man came, we went down to only 4 medicines. Now we're picking up our medicines again. So we're back up to about 28 medicines now. But me, myself, I only carry 4 medicines.

If you put all these medicines together into one pharmaceutical department, I divide them into only two classes. One class is the medicines to alleviate worries, sadness, problems, sickness, and death. They just temporarily alleviate those like nothing ever happened. Then you want to see soap bubbles and rainbow colors. You call it going on a trip. So you float around there, and you could be ten persons at the same time. Part of you is standing in L.A., part of you is standing in Chicago, and part of you is in New York. Like that. Then your body is wandering around. "What happened to my spirit?" You could be at ten places all at the same time, but your body is wandering around, see?

Then the other class is to block off all future. There's no future. That drug will bring you back to maybe four or five years old. Then you watch those little cartoons, like Star Wars or cowboys and Indians. Like John Wayne fires his little six-shooter twenty times and knocks the Indians off the horses. Everybody roots for John Wayne. So that drug will bring you back. All the bad things that you witnessed and heard, you are going to reenact. You are going to reenact all those crimes. So there are two classes of drugs. So I explained all of this when I visited the surgeon general's office.

So it's really funny how the Earth People talk. There is an everyday language, but the spiritual language I speak is different. When the spirits talk, they speak really deep. Really deep! When they gave me that power I could also speak and understand that spiritual language. So those people on the surface, they speak shallow. Their minds are really shallow, and their thinking is light.

I was told by the old people that when you hold that Chanunpa there will be bad words and thoughts blowing towards you. Like, a bad thought will come in through this room and go out. Such thoughts and words that come to you are shallow. That's what the spirit told them. They're shallow and light. They're nothing. They are like little shadows that come. But if you connect yourself with a quick thought, that will take you someplace where you will never find your way back. You will be totally lost. The old people told us that. Or, if you do find your way back, you'll be missing part of your mind or part of your body. Maybe you will lose an arm or part of your leg. Part of you will be missing. The old people told us that. But most people went that way, and now they're lost. So I learned not to connect myself with a quick thought. If those bad words come, I let them come in one ear and go out the other. I never let them come out of my mouth. If a bad word comes in your ear and then comes out of your mouth, it will go someplace and hurt somebody. If I did that, that hurt would come back twice as hard on me.

Now, talking about people getting lost, the spirit came in and told us that there are people walking around here. You see them walking around or moving around, moving about—slow pace or medium or fast pace. Sometimes they go through here real fast, and you can't see who they are. You just see something go by fast, so you can't identify what they look like. Sometimes they go slow enough that a camera could catch them. If they go real slow, you think they are harmless, but it's just as deadly as the medium or fast. So the spirit told us that there are these two-leggeds moving about here. They're moving around, but they are dead. That's what he said. So there are a lot of two-leggeds walking around here that are dead. They are already dead. So some people walk around, and they are already dead. Their senses are dead, and they don't know about these sacred powers.

To get to these sacred powers you have to go through four stages. When you reach the top, the spirit will come and communicate with you. He will give you your instructions. That's the first power, and it takes four years to acquire it. Then you go another four stages to get the second power. And there's a third power and a fourth power, see? Each of them requires four years. So that is four times four years, or sixteen years, before you reach all the way through and obtain the real power. That is the first level of power. Then there is a second level of power. That also takes sixteen years. Then there is a third and fourth level of power. So you have to go on vision quest after vision quest. The spirit will give you instructions. As you go, you go deeper and deeper. Eventually, you will be there with them. When you pass the fourth level of power you will be in the hands of the Creator, and you'll be back in Grandmother's arms again. So a lot of people come to me and want this power right now. But it's not that way. I have one more vision quest to perform, and then I will have the fourth and final power. That is the impenetrable medicine. It can cure any disease known to man. So you have to have a lot of patience for this.

The last two vision quests I went on I prayed for all those bones collected in the Smithsonian and across the board in every museum. When those spirits came, there were countless people all the way around. Each group spoke a different language, but they changed me so quick I was able to speak their language and understand each group. Next there was a big thunder and flash of lightning, and they were all gone. Everything was gone. But they said they were spirits. They had come to help me. So they thanked me for remembering them. So all these people came from all over the world and converged here. So they came this way to help me.

Then I heard the loudest voice I have ever heard in my life. The voice said, "Grandchild, I stand here watching and listening to you. Everything that you said is true. That will be so." That is what the voice said. So I was really glad. "Hey, somebody's here. Somebody's watching and listening." Then somebody said, "Now, Tunkashila is going to visit you." I heard this voice, and I heard his footsteps, but I never saw him. Then I went into this lodge and sat down. Somebody was sitting on the south side facing west. He was to my left. So I sat there for awhile waiting to see what he had to say. But he didn't speak. He didn't say anything. So I began to pray. So I kept on going. I was praying and praying. I prayed to the Four Directions, the universal prayer, to the West, North, East, and South. Then I prayed upward to the Eagle Nation and downward to the stone-people. Then in a circle to the *Eagle Bundle,* the nation's robe. When I finished, he said, "Oh, good. That is good. That is so." That's what he said. Then he said, *"Yanka."* (That means, "One moment," or to hold or pause.) I answered, "Ho." He got up and went to the door. Then he went a little ways and disappeared. So I was sitting there waiting. That is what he said to do. But I was getting impatient because he had disappeared, and I felt empty. My ears started ringing. Then there was a sound in the silence. It was a silent sound in the silence. So I got up and went out. I prayed to the Four Directions, then up and down. I made my prayer again, but he didn't come back. So I had an empty feeling.

Anyway, I prayed again. Then I came back into the lodge. I sat down way in the back. I was holding the Chanunpa, and I started to pray inside. When I finished my prayer, he was sitting right next to me. He put his arm around my shoulder and kind of assured me that everything was okay. Then he rocked me. He was flesh and bones to assure me that he was there.

That was the first time. I had heard his footsteps and heard his voice many times before in my life, but I never saw him. But this time, now he appeared. I didn't see him come in, but he appeared right beside me. He had one arm around my shoulder, and he held his other hand on my hand and the Chanunpa.

He said, "My name is Invisible Walks."

I answered, "Oh, thank you."

Then he disappeared right there. But I felt comfortable because I knew that he was there. He appeared and disappeared, but I knew he was close by me. So, Invisible Walks, that was his name. It was the first time I saw him. You could hear his footsteps and hear him talk, but you couldn't see him. Even the stone-people, stone-man couldn't detect him. So he was invisible to the spirits, too!

Then the other Thunder Spirit came. I was on a mountain, and the clouds below me were like the land. He walked on those clouds, and there was thunder and lightning. When he landed on the mountaintop, the whole mountain started moving. It was shaking. When he took a step, big rocks cracked underneath his feet and started rolling down the mountain—boom, boom, like that. So it must have been a tremendous weight, because the whole mountain shook and big boulders cracked. It must have been tons and tons.

I was scared to look at him. He was lightning all over. His face, hands, everything was lightning. He came from West, and lightning also came with him. That lightning went right into the bowl of the Chanunpa I was holding and came out the mouthpiece. It made a loud explosion like a gun. It did that four times. I still have lightning burns, scorch burns, on that Chanunpa stem. That's why we wrap the stem with sage. That sage kept me from getting electrocuted. That sage is like clouds. A piece of sage is a piece of cloud. So I insulated that Chanunpa stem with clouds.

Maybe I'm dumb. I was just standing there watching all of this. Maybe if I had had a little sense I would have thrown down the Chanunpa and taken off. If some five-year-old kid went there and heard that boom, he'd yell "Mommy! Mommy!" Like that. Maybe a five-year-old kid would have sense enough to run, but I just stood there wondering what was going to happen to me next. So I continued to pray.

It was pitch dark, but I saw him move around. Then a light came all around me. Even the robes [ceremonial flags] lit up. I could even see the stitches, like magnifying. I could see the green [plants]. I could see pine needles. Then he moved his arms, and there was a wall of darkness all around me. Then he opened it, like pulling back a curtain, and I could see medicine-people— plants [of one species]. He said, "There will be a time when you need help. These medicine-people are going to help you." So when I looked over there in the pitch dark I could see those plants standing right there. So I picked one and brought it back. I didn't recognize it. That way, I knew what it looked like. When I went back, I looked around, and I saw the imposters—those look-alikes. But I knew what the real medicine looked like because I brought it back with me from that vision.

There were people down below on the mountain that had come there to help and watch over me on my vision quest. When they saw all this lightning, they got scared also. One of those bolts of lightning went down there and went right through the lodge. Went right through them. It was really hot. There was a big ball in the front—purple, green, orange—and it was really hot. Some of those people standing there got wringing wet, it was so hot.

Pretty soon a tall spirit came there. He told them to go pick me up because the spirits were going to take me to West, and they were not going to bring me back [meaning he was going to die]. So everybody prayed. Then they came up the mountain and told me they had come to pick me up. They said that a tall spirit had told them to come for me because the spirits were going to take me to where West ends—back to my mom and dad and to see my grandpa again. So two of them started to help me down the mountain because they thought I was weak and tired. Then they both slipped and fell. Whoops. So I picked them up again. So I'm the one who holds them up. They laughed.

So I learned a lot from the spirits that way. So I bring this medicine to the ceremony and tie it there. Then that spirit is around some place. So I say, "Yo-ho," and he comes in. So we have a medicine man that comes in. He never carries a knife and carves out your heart, throws it away, and then takes somebody else's heart or a baboon's heart in there. He doesn't use an artificial heart either. We have one medicine man that comes in that does four things. He's a blood doctor. He's a bone doctor. He's a sinew doctor. You might call him a neurologist, because he recreates the nerves. And he talks and untangles your mind. He sets your mind straight—Four Directions, up and down, then in a circle, see?

We asked the spirit once how come people got so confused. One person came there for help. He had a headache for four years. They gave him all kinds of medicines, but it was still there. So we asked the spirit about that. He said it was like you take a subject. Then you string it across your mind. Then you take another subject. Then you string it across your mind. All those subjects overlap, and their ends are imbedded in your mind. Then there's another one on top of that. So after education, it becomes like a cobweb in there. But all of these subjects are not connected. They just overlap and tangle your mind. They are embedded deep in your mind. When you try to connect them together, you become confused and get a headache. So the spirit told us that.

When that spirit comes in, he untangles all of this and sets your mind straight. He eases your mind, and your headache goes away. He comes in by talking. He untangles and sets you straight; so you might call him a psychiatrist or psychologist. But we have a psychologist. He's a spirit. Those other psychologists, they can't do anything because their mind is tangled also.

So I learned all this from the Chanunpa. It takes prayers. It takes a lot of work. It takes a lot of courage. It takes a lot of patience. It takes a lot of endurance. So you could practice. You could rest your tummy for four days and see how it feels, because that's how many days you are going to go vision quest. Ninety-six hours is a mighty stretch! But what's really going to get you down like nothing is when you start thinking about time. When you go to Tunkashila, there is no time. There's no past or present or future time. Everything is the same. So when you understand that, then Earth time is nothing. It will just fly by you. You won't even know about it. But if you go there and start thinking about time, you're dead.

So it's going to take you eight years before you really understand what I am saying. What I'm telling you now is just like elementary class, like kindergarten stuff. So you can't understand everything in just three or four hours, or one day. And I'm trying to speak really simple English so any five-year-old could understand what I'm saying. It's really hard because you are all full of anticipation. You jump to a conclusion before a paragraph is finished, and then you end up with a blank. Then afterwards you question—Why? Why? Why? That confuses you. When that spirit comes, we don't ever ask questions. If I don't understand, I just hold onto it. Then later down the road, maybe in a couple of years, I understand what that spirit meant.

CHAPTER 4

The Chanunpa

The Chanunpa is where I go to school. You see the same thing over and over. I've been going back and forth here for sixty-three years because I've been taught by the Chanunpa. I'm sixty-eight now, so it's been going on for sixty-three years. So I've got just a little jiffy time there, but I sure learned a lot in that little jiffy time. It's good. So all of you who have been educated, you should be able to understand the way of the Chanunpa more than what I learned in the little jiffy time spent here.

Right now the Chanunpa, the spirit is kind of wedging its way, finding its way gradually. Sometimes it stops. Then it goes. You never use force. It has to do with the way people move and pray. We pierce in the Sun Dance or go without food or water in order to contact spirit. When that spirit comes, we have all the chance in the world. We could say anything we want there. So I have to prepare myself to be alert as to what I say, what I've been longing to say all my life.

I want to say a lot of things, but I have no one to tell it to. I reported to my senators and congressmen, but they don't have money, and they don't have time for that. They are always counting money first. It seems that they have more important things to talk about than my little worries and sadness and pain and death. But I think we are up against the wall now and have no alternative but to turn to the American Indians. So I think we are at a turning point now. So there's a hope. There's a chance.

The Earth People are rooted in the fire, rock, water, and green. The problem, the saddest part for this society is that if we were to go back to this Earth People philosophy there is no money there. That is really hard for people to understand. It's the saddest part for them, but they have to understand the power of this Chanunpa. One time I was holding this Chanunpa, and the fire came. That power came from the sun. Then the spirit said, "Tunkashila hears you, so he sent me here." Then he talked about a little tiny fire. "This fire that I brought here, I will call it the impenetrable medicine. Now I put this impenetrable medicine in the bottom of the bowl of that Chanunpa you are holding. It is *wakan* [holy]. I will place it there. So from this bowl through that little tunnel to the mouthpiece of the Chanunpa you will escape with countless people from this nuclear holocaust." So that was his promise. So every time I fill the Chanunpa I look in there and see that light. Then I know the prayer is going to be good.

When we place that medicine, that tobacco in there, it attracts electricity. So you see those lights come in during the ceremony. There are a lot of things you people have to learn. You have to start over again. So I'll put you all back into kindergarten, but this time you're not going to see a dog jump and say "Arf! Arf!" This time you're actually going to hear it talk and learn how to sniff. You're going to learn how to hear, how to taste, and how to feel. You're not just going to rely on your naked eyes. We overload our naked eyes. We overload that little computer chip, so the wires short out. There's an electrical storm going around in our head. So we have a big storm going on in our head. So we have to stay close together and stay behind this Chanunpa. Never sidestep it or go along the side. Don't go in front of it. Let the Chanunpa always lead. That's the instruction that we carry. And that Chanunpa will lead us to safety where there is no end— where there's happiness and joy. There's no pain. There's no death. There won't be anybody coming around to collect rent or taxes or anything. Eventually, the Chanunpa will lead us all back into the hands of Tunkashila. Grandmother, she will cradle us again. She knows that we have been naughty kids, but instead of spanking us, she'll wipe our tears and forgive us. They are the only ones that could forgive. Instead of punishing us, they'll forgive us. So the real amnesty is there. We know that. So don't be afraid. What we left behind, leave it back there. Try to do some good. Let's try to take a step, try to think something good. Try to take a step in a good way. So that is my prayer.

You have to understand this Chanunpa. When we say *Chanunpa,* that's what it means. *Cha* is "a wood." *Nunpa* is "two." The bowl represents the whole world. The stem represents the Tree of Life. Then there is the main Chanunpa. That Chanunpa was first brought to us by the White Buffalo-Calf Maiden. We still carry that original Chanunpa. Orval Looking Horse is the keeper of that Chanunpa. That Chanunpa is like a radio, like a radar. You could communicate from here directly to that main Chanunpa. You could communicate directly with the wisdom. Like I said, Tunkashila is the wisdom itself, and Grandmother is the knowledge.

The buffalo gave his life so we could wear his robe. His blood sifted into the ground and became a stone. So we have a red stone. Also, we have a black stone. That stone represents the universe. It represents the woman. The Tree of Life, the stem part, is the man. So male and female are connected together in that Chanunpa. That spells generation because of the fire, rock, water, and green. So the Chanunpa is very sacred. We didn't carve it; Tunkashila carved it. Then he offered it to his people. So this is the power. So the Chanunpa is sacred of sacreds in the whole universe. It will be known all over the world. That is in our prophecies.

So now we have stone-people-lodges everywhere. We even have one in Tokyo. So in each land, everywhere, you name it. They even have it in Communist countries. I went to East Germany and saw two hundred tipis there. It was really something. So now the Chanunpa is back there also. So it has traveled all over the world. They say this fireplace, this fire will travel all over the world. That is coming true. You find stone-people-lodges everywhere in the world now. So it will come back again, and the whole universe will be a giant stone-people-lodge. It will be a purification. So it's good to learn our ways.

All the knowledge that is floating around here between the

earth and sky was given to me free of charge. It was just given to me. And that knowledge has no end to it. This Chanunpa has no end to it, and that impenetrable medicine is in the bottom of the bowl. So I will escape with countless people from this nuclear destruction. Now I pray to the powers of the Four Winds that my people will lay this fire [nuclear weapons] down before that destruction comes.

I'm glad that there are a lot of young people carrying the Chanunpa now. You have to understand all of this. Always put your people ahead. If you take something to your mouth, always remember the spirit first. When you run into a good thing, like a T-bone steak, take a piece and remember your people first. If you have a piece of meat or a bowl of soup, you look for an elder and you look for an orphan. You feed those two. They are the most poor. They are defenseless. So these two you have to cradle in your arms, and you have to put something in their mouth first. Then Tunkashila will bless you for it, and your day will be long. These are the instructions the Chanunpa carries.

The Chanunpa carries seven rituals. There's a spiritual food-offering ceremony. It's called *wanagi*, or "soul-keeping ceremony." You keep the spirit and you feed it. Then there is the vision quest [*hanbleceya*], Sun Dance, Tossing Ball ceremony, Ghost Dance, Thunder ceremonies, and stone-people-lodge. The path is always the same. There is nothing to change. It's always the same, but today we are only carrying three of those rituals. They are like sacraments to us.

So we have to go step by step. I participate in the rituals every four years. Sometimes the going gets tough. Recently we tried to revive the Tossing Ball ceremony. We talked about those ball-tossing games they play in the schools. So that ball-tossing ceremony is really a global ceremony today. In the ritual we perform it for help and health, but the white man copied it and commercialized it. So now we have all these commercial games like soccer, football, and baseball.

So there is a lot to understand about this Chanunpa. I already told you about making the Chanunpa—how it took me four years to make my first Chanunpa. Then you have to know how to fill the Chanunpa and then how to offer it. We don't put just anything in there. We have a pipe mixture that we make. It is made from four parts red willow bark, one part tobacco, one part *kinic-kinic,* and sprinkled, like peppered, with *tobacco root.* You have to remember how much of each of these to use to make the mixture taste good. You need to know on which moon to gather each one of those plants. If you pick them too early or too late they will taste bitter. You only use certain parts. You don't use the whole plant. Like they call it red willow bark, but what you really use there is that little sheet of green in there between the bark and the wood. You have to scrape that one. Then you have to learn how to dry them and cut them. So there is a lot to learn about how to take care of the Chanunpa.

When you fill the Chanunpa, there is a pipe-filling song that goes with it. During that time everybody should respect that Chanunpa and not talk. They can sing that song if they want to. There is a certain way you put that tobacco [mixture] in there. You have to educate your fingers, your pinch, for that. The old people told me that you have to be really careful when you're accepting the Chanunpa. When you put your mixture into the bowl, you should never put bad words or bad thoughts in that offering. Don't wish bad luck or death or like that. If I hear what's in that Chanunpa, like death or bad luck for someone, I will take that Chanunpa, disconnect it, and return it to that person.

So you have to state your reason. When you offer the Chanunpa you say, "Tunkashila, I offer this Chanunpa." Then you state the reason you are offering it. "I have a dad lying in the hospital with a heart attack. Tunkashila, go there and extend my father's life another day or another moon or another year or another generation." Then you pivot and present the Chanunpa to the medicine man. The medicine man or woman will hold out hands [arms extended and palms upward]. You hold that Chanunpa level in front of you. You hold it with both hands [palms upward]. Then you place it in their hands four times. You don't let it go. You just go there with it and then pull it back. Each time you pull it back, you pray. Then on the fourth time you let it go. He will accept it. When he accepts it, everybody says, "Hi-ho! Hi-ho!" It's like you applaud. You praise, you're thankful, you cheer, you yell, like that. Maybe in Christianity they would say,

"Hallelujah. Amen." It's acceptance, because that Chanunpa is going to go before the Creator. That's the reason it's presented this way.

But like I said, if that person puts something in there that doesn't belong in there, then bad thoughts and bad words will be blowing your way. So never take one and put it in the Chanunpa. If you do that, then it is going to happen that way, but that's going to come back to you twice. Eventually, when people do something like that and leave the Chanunpa and go away, then that whole family—just one by one or all in one shot—dies.

So this Chanunpa is really sacred, and we have to be really careful how we handle it. It's not a toy when you have part of the wisdom of the Creator and the power of Grandmother, one drop from each, in your hands. The power is the atom. We call it nuclear bombs or neutron bombs or like that. But that power is in our hands. And that gift, that love, is in our hands.

A lot of Christian people try to interpret God. They say God is love or love is God, like that. People don't really understand. That Chanunpa can destroy with that bad thought or bad word in there. That is why I said that the spirit told me if a bad thought or bad word ever comes to you, to let it go in your ear and out the other ear, but never out of your mouth. If it comes out of your mouth it is going to hurt somebody, and then that hurt will come back to you twice. If you connect yourself to quick thought, that will take you someplace you'll never find your way back from. This was told many generations ago. So it was handed down. So when you have that Chanunpa, you have to be humble and sincere. You ask for *health* and *help*. These are the two key words that the Chanunpa carries.

That Chanunpa will serve you many times—not just one time, but many times. So that is why the Chanunpa is *wakan*. The spirit will come and tell you the Chanunpa is *wakan*. You had better start praying because that is a warning. That doesn't mean that it's a cure-all or you have a safety insurance. It's not that way. It's a warning. Then you have to pray. So I began to wonder about that, and I asked Tunkashila, "How come the spirit comes in and tells us that Chanunpa is *wakan?*" I asked the spirit that question. Then I learned the answer. When a person prays, that power goes back to the Creator. Even if you misinterpret or mistranslate something that doesn't belong to you, or it doesn't belong to the Chanunpa, or it doesn't belong to the Creator or Grandmother, then some unknown power will destroy that. The way he said it was, "If a bad thought or word comes, you pray, and that bad thought or word will turn around. It will go back to the mouth where it came out from. It will go back to the mouth, and it will go back to earth along with the robe, the body. Then, the shadow of that man will be standing there. So then that bad thought or word will return to earth. Then there will be nothing; so the body will deteriorate."

So one of my people had a question. "If we carry this Chanunpa, what will happen if we drink alcohol and take drugs?" The spirit answered. He mentioned a cloth. He said your robe [body] is like a piece of cloth. So when you put alcohol and drugs in there it will go back to earth again, because this medicine is sacred. So when that person takes it, he'll go back to earth. So here is your robe. If you pour it on this cloth, it will seep right through and will return to earth. That cloth will start to fall apart, and it will be back to earth. So when you drink and take all those pills, your body will deteriorate, and it will go back to earth.

Then your shadow will be standing there, wandering and floating around. "What happened to my robe? It's dirt." Then you will see the wonders and mysteries of Tunkashila. You are going to see that *black light.* You are going to see all those creatures around you. We don't see them, but they see us. You see your people here, but they can't see you. So you go back to the breath of spirit. It remains here, because the wisdom [from Tunkashila] and knowledge [from Grandmother] were placed here. It doesn't go anywhere; it just stays right here.

So we were told that way. So the spirit that we are talking about, it is a great mystery. Like this air. It is here. You can see it moving the grass and leaves around. You can feel it, but you can't see it with your naked eyes. But it's here, and we are all breathing it, whether it's a black man or red man or yellow man or white man or winged, four-legged, creeping-crawler, mammal, or fish-people. We are all breathing the same air. So that's just an example of how spirit goes back to spirit. This is the way it was told. So I pray this wind will blow away piece by piece those bad thoughts coming our way.

So you could pray to this wind. Maybe you have a problem in your head because, like they say in the medical science, a virus is going around. So you take an aspirin. But aspirin doesn't purify the air. It removes your headache, but it doesn't clear the virus away. But those creatures over there, every day they nibble and drink water. So they are still able to communicate with those powers. They are here twenty-four hours around the clock. They are much closer than us two-leggeds, because we lost that communication. So what we do is to ask for help from one of those creatures, like the deer, through this Chanunpa. We have a deer medicine. Each creature has a medicine, so there are many medicines. Because they are so close to the Creator, they are able to communicate that medicine. Then they bring help and health.

Our minds are contaminated. So the Earth and its creatures are also contaminated. When a deer gets a headache, well, he goes to that medicine, and he prays. He nibbles on that green and drinks water. When he lies down, that medicine goes all the way around and clears out all the virus. So all those little guys [fawns] jumping around there, they also benefit because one deer prayed. So we borrow that medicine from the deer. So he brings that medicine. Then it clears our head. It not only clears the headache, it also clears the virus causing the headache so it doesn't go around in my family. Then it doesn't come to us. It goes away. So that's just one medicine. That's just an example of what we call deer medicine.

So it is a spirit. So they bring those powers in a certain way. Through the Chanunpa, tobacco ties, and robes, you call them. Then they come in and wear those robes. They're standing there watching you. So when those stone-people become alive again, they come in [to the stone-people-lodge]. Then you visit with them and tell them your problems. Then the power that pollutes our mind is released. That fire will come in and destroy bad thoughts and words. Only good thoughts and words will remain. To that the spirit adds power and returns it to us. That's what the spirit does—the stone-people, fire, rock, and water.

So there is a ritual you have to follow. Never do it on your own. You always have to have a spirit guide. When you go there, when you have the fire and the stone-people, you offer a little green and water to them. Then, through this Chanunpa, somebody is listening to you, somebody is watching you. When you go there you have to have *courage, patience, endurance, and alertness.* These four you have to have. If you are missing one of them, that's your weak spot. So you have to have all four of them to be an Earth Man. So you are going to develop. You are going to educate yourself. You are going to exercise and develop this power in yourself. So if you're not really sure, then test yourself through spring, summer, fall, and winter. So you might go all four seasons around. Then you might try another round. You might go around four times before you reaffirm, rededicate yourself. Then you go in a humble way. Then Tunkashila will pity you. He'll come, but he is going to test you first. He might even test you three or four times.

For example, I have a nephew that just went on his vision quest. When the powers came, a man came to him. He said, "There's a creature coming. You'd better pick up your Chanunpa and just take off now. Go home because there's a four-legged that's going to come and kill you. So you'd better take off now." So he tried to pray. Then he heard something growling—grrrr, grrrr. It was getting louder and louder and echoed. He got goose pimples all over, and his hair was standing up. Then he saw it. It was a big grizzly bear! He came over and stood up. He towered over ten or eleven feet high. Way up there!

So my nephew fell down, holding his Chanunpa, and started to pray. Then there was a man touching him who said, "Oh, we thank you son. You are true. You came and humbled yourself, so I'm going to help you." So that bear came to his altar and helped him. He gave him the medicine. Then he said, "Whenever you need help, call on me. I'll come to help you. Any one of your relatives come here dying through his last breath with lungs collapsed, he'll be breathing with this moccasin lung." So they called it "moccasin lung." So when your two lungs collapse, you could still be breathing on this moccasin lung. Then he said, "I will come and I will rescue him. I will make him walk to his loved ones in good health and spirit. Remember that. I am a spirit. I'm sacred. So we come here to give you health and help."

Then my nephew thanked him, and he left. So he had that medicine in his hand. When I went to the vision quest site after him, he had that root in his hand. So he came back with that root in his hand. Now, whenever he wants to use it, he takes part of it and ties it onto the Chanunpa then, "Yo-ho," sends a voice in Four Directions. Then somebody over there answers him. That is science. That is the way you catch the power.

So we rely on this medicine. We rely on these creatures, their ingenuity and powers. They even send a voice to the Creator for us, because we don't have an amplifier. We don't have a radio to send a message way up there. We may be able to send a little gadget to Mars, but we never send a voice to the Creator. We never say, "Hey, Grandfather, where are you? How are you? From up there, how do we look down here?" So we can't do that. We can't send an electrical wave up there, and five years later a message will come back. It's not that way. But over here, the Earth People say, "Yo-ho," and somebody answers back, "Yes. What do you want?" That is science. So we don't have to wait five years for some higher intelligence to send a message back.

This Chanunpa is our relative. So we're not orphans. We have Tunkashila and Grandmother here. The power is here. It is in our hands, so we have to take good care of it. I can remember how my grandmother cared for the Chanunpa. Whenever she took that Chanunpa into her arms, she always cradled it like a baby. Sometimes she would rock with the Chanunpa in her arms and sing lullabies to it and pray to it. She would pray for her grandchildren, and it always happened the way she prayed.

That Chanunpa gives comfort also. Sometimes in our ceremonies we use drums. So there is a lot of banging and noise going on, but our kids are all there sleeping away. One time that noise bothered our neighbor. Those white children heard that big drum, and they got scared because they didn't know what was going on. So we prayed to the spirit to go over there and comfort those little people. They did that. So now when they hear that drum they get up and start dancing around. They put two fingers up behind their head like feathers and start dancing around. Now they feel good. Those kids got smart, because their mind wasn't really polluted yet. So it's free. So they could feel it. They could feel the spirit.

So this Chanunpa is for everyone. Don't ever call it Black Elk's Chanunpa. Never say it that way. This Chanunpa belongs to you people. It belongs to the nation. It takes a lot of power. It takes years and years. So it takes stages to attain this power. So this Chanunpa is not mine. It belongs to the people. But with this Chanunpa, I could see the whole world. It tells me what is happening, what is going on. It's like little moving pictures going on.

So in order to understand this sacred Chanunpa, you have to understand that it is a way of life. Someone asked me once if they had to have a Chanunpa before they joined the "Sacred Pipe religion," but it's not that way. It's not an organized church. It's not an Indian religion. It is a way of life. So that's how come I'm odd. I'm different. I'm totally different from other people. So I want to explain that way to you. When you come from that university to the lodge, you're back in kindergarten.

So the spirits say that Tunkashila, the power, is a lightning. There is a trail alongside this lightning. We travel, we run and walk, alongside the lightning. So there are trails alongside the clouds. We have trails alongside the clouds. So the Thunder Spirits told me that. There's a song. They sang that song. They said, "We carry this power. When we go across this land, we look down, and wherever there is a cedar or sage burned or wherever we see tobacco ties and robes, that is where we go take a pause and break. We look there. Whatever they ask for, we help. Then we go over or we split, each goes around or goes to one side." That's what they said.

Now to the center of this Chanunpa. The center is the Earth, and on this Earth we build the stone-people-lodge. It's a little dome. Inside we poke a little hole in the center into the earth so the spirit could breathe and talk. Then we bring offerings. We offer green—cedar, sage, and sweetgrass. We fill the Chanunpa and offer it. We offer tobacco ties. They are our prayers. We offer robes [strips of colored cotton]. The spirits read those ties and wear those robes. We offer sacred food of water, corn, berries, and meat. We offer the stone-people that contain that fire. And the best offering we bring there is ourselves. So when you offer your robe and commit your spirit to the Creator, that is the highest offering. That way Tunkashila is pleased. Then the spirit comes and says, "You did good. You did well. Keep it up. Keep coming. Stay on this path. You'll make it. You'll make it home. You'll reach that destiny."

That destiny is all your time, all your life, generation after generation. You teach your children, then you die. You're in spirit now. Then you will see what you sowed. It's rising. It's growing. So you die, but your seed, your bone, your blood, your spirit, is still going. So it goes on and on, generation after generation. So we're going in that direction all the time, no matter what the odds are against us. Like here in the United States, it's like 230 million people against one Indian. That's a tremendous odd. They could do anything they want. They could instantly do away with us. But some mysterious way, they can't get rid of us. Somehow, there's some reason that keeps us alive.

So there is a lot to learn about the stone-people-lodge. We place those robes in the stone-people-lodge. When you go there you will see colored robes hanging there—black for West, red for North, yellow for East, white for South, blue for sky, and green for earth. Never call them flags, because they are robes. *Shina* is the Lakota word for them. That means "blanket, robe." So the spirit comes and wears those robes. They watch you and listen to you. So the robe Tunkashila and Grandmother gave you, you call your birthday suit. So we don't call our birthday suit *flag.* We call it *robe,* and your spirit wears it. So you have a spirit that wears this robe, and it carries a communication center that is centered in your heart. So you have to have a heart first. Then you have to have courage, patience, endurance, and alertness. That is what you have to have to be an Earth Man.

Besides these robes, we also have a nations robe that we use in the stone-people-lodge ceremony. It is made of pure wool and is red. Grandmother, she wears this red wool. To that we tie a feather and a *pearl* [a circular piece of pink conch shell about one and a half inches in diameter]. That pearl comes from the bottom of the ocean. That feather hanging there is an eagle feather. He flies the highest. So we connect the highest and the lowest together. The origin of the human cell begins from this pearl. It is the woman, and birth begins from there. So when a girl turns into a woman we have a ceremony where she stands backwards on one of those pearls. Also, she is decorated with a plume, a feather on top of her head. The old people told us that when the sun comes up there is a star there at daybreak. So Tunkashila wears a plume on top of his head, and this plume is called the *anpo wie* [morning star]. It is a "dawn light." *Wie* means "light" or "sun." So it is the "morning sun." So this feather that the girl wears on top of her head is *anpo wie.* So that light is around her all the time.

So you need to use those robes when you want to have a ceremony. It is part of our sacred ways. We also display those tobacco ties there. The spirit will tell you how many ties and what colors to use. For my altar I normally use one string of 50 ties and another string of 150 ties—all red. For special ceremonies we use other colors. Then we have the sacred food there also. We always place that in wooden bowls. It is best to use new wooden bowls or bowls that have only been used for sacred food. There are special ways to prepare that food also. For example, we use calico corn that is ground up and mixed with suet and raisins for the corn offering. The water should come from a spring. However, there are times that we are forced to use substitutes. Sometimes we have to get water from the faucet or open a can of corn and dump it in. For the berries, we try to use chokecherries, but if they are not available we might have to use a can of blueberries instead. If we don't have dried meat, we might have to open up a can of corned beef or something like that. We use whatever we can get because we are poor and pitiful.

So we use these offerings for the stone-people-lodge ceremony. Then that spirit comes in. So we don't have a communication problem. I could talk to those spirits. Each one has a language. If you hear them speak, you won't understand what they say because they use a secret and sacred code. It is a scientific language. It's Lakota. That's how come it's really hard for me to translate into English. Take the word *mni. Mni* is the Lakota word for water. *Ni* means the "breath of life," so *mni* identifies that water is life—living water. Water is a living. But in English the word *water* doesn't say that it is living or anything; water is just water. But in Lakota it is identified with the life.

So when that gourd comes into the lodge, he talks. All you are going to hear is a sound that sounds like a baby rattle flying around in there. But those stones in that gourd talk. There is a talk in that rattle, but you have to be educated in these spiritual ways to understand it. Other times you will see those little lights flashing around in the dark. I have a medicine for that. It comes from the stones. The first time they gave me those stones, there was a thunder and a lightning. A flash of light came right through the lodge and somebody jumped in. He said, "I'm a stone-man. I give you this power." So I carry this little medicine. It attracts electricity. It attracts lightning. So when I use this stone, these lights come. They talk like little radio waves. If you keep your eyes open, you'll see different lights in the pitch dark, the black light. You'll see yellow or red or some other color inside. So this is just one little mystery.

So we do have medicine men that come in. Each one has a name. They identify themselves. Like I have one whose name is Rings-in-the-water. I have another one named Fast and another one named Invisible Walks. I have many that come in. So we know them like we know people. So once you get used to it, you make a lot of acquaintances. You make a lot of relations. So you learn from the Chanunpa. It is sacred. Nobody can predict when, where, or how they are going to come, or how they are going to test you. For example, we had this white man who almost caught a spirit. He came over to the Rocky Mountains for a vision quest, and the spirits tested him. Now that word *vision quest*, it belongs to the *wasichu* [white man]. So that word doesn't belong to us. We have a different word. We use the word *hanbleceya*. *Hanhepi* is the night. *Ble* is where it's quiet. That's where a person comes with pain and tears to plea for something. So I don't think there's a word in the whole English language that could accurately define *hanbleceya*.

So when he went to *hanbleceya* he wasn't thinking right. You have to be prepared. Sometimes when a person commits himself to *hanbleceya* it takes him at least four years to prepare for it. You don't just go there, and somebody brings you a bowl of food every day. You don't just sit out there and daydream. That's not a vision quest. But this guy, he went to sleep. He has to get his

eight hours of sleep, then up at six o'clock, do his chores—pray
to the Four Directions, then up and down, then a circle, then he's
finished. It was like that. So that's the way he had planned it. He
grew up that way, so he wants to plan according to the way he
trained all his life. So he lay down and kept a hold of his Chanunpa. That was the one thing he remembered. I told him to
never let go of his Chanunpa during the vision quest, and so he
hung onto it. But if you go to sleep there, you won't know
anything. You don't go there to sleep. When you go on your
vision quest, you don't go there to sleep. Some people say, "Well,
what about if you want to go to the toilet?" Well, you don't go
there to go to the toilet either. You go there to pray. You don't
go there to sleep, or it will be all gone.

So he started going to bed, and somebody hit the top of his
vision quest lodge. Two hands were banging on it several times.
So he started yelling—"Who the hell are you? What do you
want?"—instead of praying to Tunkashila for health and help.
He should have said, "Please do come in. Tunkashila, please hear
my prayers," instead of saying, "What do you want? Who's out
there?" So you have to be ready. You have to be humble.

Then it was quiet. No footsteps. No sound. Now he swore that
before he went in he saw a tree standing there. But he's on top
of the mountain, and the trees don't grow up there. So it's bare.
But before he came into the lodge he thought he saw a tree
standing there, so he thought it must have been a chipmunk that
came down from that tree and bounced around on the top of the
lodge and then went back up into that tree. He imagined it that
way.

So he started going back to bed again. He had to get his sleep.
About the time he got himself all tucked in, two hands started
rolling back and forth together in the dark. They made that sound
in there. "Who's in here? What do you want? Who are you?"
Then he swore that somebody stuck his hand through the top of
the lodge while holding a flashlight. We talked about those lights.
Then the light went out. So he started feeling around to see if
there was a hole in the top of that lodge. But there was no hole.
In fact, he built that lodge himself, so there was no hole in it.

So now he got scared. So he laid his Chanunpa down and

started crawling around in there to see if he could feel anybody or anything. When he came back around to where he laid the Chanunpa down, his Chanunpa was gone. Now, that's even more scary! So he rolled up his blanket and put it around his neck and started all over again. He started feeling all around, inch by inch, wall to wall, like that. Nothing. So now he's scared to stay in there, and he's scared to go outside. So he prayed and prayed and prayed. Then he saw a little light. Pretty soon he heard birds, and he could see those tobacco ties laying out there around the lodge. So he came out and was ready to make a beeline back to the stone-people-lodge where he started.

I got there just in time. The spirit came and warned me, "That man is about ready to take off." So I prayed, "Hold him there until I get there." So when I got there, his eyes were really big. He started saying, "I can't take it any more. I'm not ready. I'm not prepared for this. I can't bear to think about another day and night here. Take me back." He was talking like that. So I prayed. Then I rolled up the tobacco ties into a ball and placed them on the altar. Then I opened up the lodge, prayed, and went in. I looked up, and his Chanunpa and Chanunpa bag were tucked between the ribs of the lodge and the lodge covers. So I pulled it out and came out. He said, "Where was it? Where did you find it?" and like that.

So I prayed and laid the Chanunpa across the altar on top of some sage. I laid it there to finish his commitment, because the Chanunpa is sacred. But the Chanunpa carrier had failed, so I brought this man back. The next day, I went back up there. I rolled all the ties and robes together in a bundle and left them up there. I brought his Chanunpa back to him. Then we wiped it. Then I reloaded his Chanunpa for him. Then we smoked it and left. So those are things I have to go through. You have to be really alert all the time about how you handle this Chanunpa. You never use your own judgment. You don't add anything to it. It is best to get your instructions from the spirits. Listen to the spirit. That's the correct way. Then you won't confuse anyone, and you won't confuse yourself either.

But me, I'm very pitiful. I am a poor boy, yet I'm rich in spiritual power, spiritual knowledge. I want to give it back free, because you can't value this power in terms of money. That's impossible. You could melt all the gold in the world, and it would not buy one drop of this knowledge. So I want to stay behind this sacred Chanunpa. I want that Chanunpa to be my best friend. In Lakota, to make a friend is the hardest. That's the toughest job. Once you make a friend, a friend never leaves you, even to death. So a friend is really hard to find. Really hard! So if you want to make a friend to those powers, to make a friend to that eagle or bear or like that, that is going to be hard. You can't just walk up and shake hands, "How do you do, friend." That bear is going to growl at you. You're going to have a little shadow of a doubt, and then you're contaminated. He might sniff at you once, then he'll growl at you or take off. You can't just go over and shake hands with him. So you have to pack a rifle or wear a cross around your neck. But that doesn't really guarantee whether or not you have a friend. Without those it's really tough to make a friend.

So my grandfather told me never to make a friend. If you're going to make a friend, do it right. He said there were two kinds of friends. Not just one friend, but there are two friends. One is a friendly enemy, and the other is the real friend. So he told us that. So never make friends until you know how. If you understand, if you are ready to give your robe, commit your spirit to the powers of Tunkashila and Grandmother, then you are able to make a friend. Otherwise, you're going to make a friendly enemy. You're going to make an enemy.

If you study history real good you'll see that we made treaties by shaking hands and making friends to the white man. So they became friendly enemies. Like in World War II, I tried to be patriotic. I joined the biggest gang fight in the world. I lived through to tell about it. I was in for four years, from Pearl Harbor in 1941 to the end of the war in 1945. The war was officially over on September 2, and four days later, on September 6, I was discharged. I carry an honorable discharge and all of the medals except the Congressional Medal of Honor. So I lived through the whole war. I came home with a lot of holes in my buckskin, but it's a good thing I didn't lose an arm or leg.

My people prayed for me and prayed for our country in the war. President Roosevelt requested that my grandfather pray with the Chanunpa. He said that all religions had to pray together. So he just said heck to the laws, rules, and regulations. We didn't know how long that war was going to last or how many millions of people would die. They even thought that we might run out of resources and that people would be starving to death and killing each other. So it was requested that we use our Chanunpa. So my people went up to the mountain and prayed with the Chanunpa. The spirit told them that the war would go on for four years before coming to an end. Four years later, on that same day, they went back up to the mountain to pray for four days. On the fourth day, the last day, the war ended. So those spirits helped us win that war.

CHAPTER 5

The Stone-People-Lodge

They have people that come around now and then to investigate me. One time these two guys came and said they were Indian research people. They even showed me their papers. So I told them to come on in. They asked me if they could use a tape recorder, and I said that was great. I like that science and technology because this is where it all began. We kept the original science and technology—the fire, rock, water, and green.

So they kept asking what's this and what's that. So I tried to explain things to them real simple, like you would to a two-year-old kid.

"Well, what's this?"

"Well, that is what you call fire."

"What's that?"

"Well, that is a rock."

"What kind of rock?"

"Well, it's a lava rock. Lava comes down and cools off, and then we put the fire back into those rocks."

He'd write all this stuff down. It seemed like they didn't know anything, so it was really hard for me to educate them. It seemed like I would have to take them all over the mountains, across the rivers, and like that. These guys were from the high intelligence people, so they needed to write everything down. They probably came from Harvard University where John Harvard put together the science, psychology, legal, and religious languages. People who get educated speak one of those languages. But there was one thing that John Harvard left out, and that was spirit. So I had to explain everything in detail to these guys.

They asked me, "Can we take pictures?"

I said, "Sure. Go ahead, if you can't memorize it." I know these guys went to school and learned to memorize seventy-five new words a week, but here they can't even remember six colors and where they go. So they should have that Polaroid camera to record which directions those colors go or tattoo it on their arm or stomach so they won't forget.

So we were getting ready to go into the stone-people-lodge. Well, they wanted to know what happens in there. I told them that a spirit comes in. So they wanted to take pictures, and I told them it would be better for them to just crawl in. Then they wanted to know how hot it gets in there. I told them that if they have straight hair it will curl it or if they have curly hair it will straighten it. That's how hot it gets. Anyway, they decided to crawl in there with us.

Then that spirit came in in that black light. He told me that these two guys were really two-faced and that they came here just to investigate me. Then that spirit said that he was also a detective, an investigator, and that he was going to teach them about the spirit. He said he would teach them so they would never forget.

So I told these guys that they were two-faced, and they admitted to being undercover agents. They said they had been sent to investigate the "Sacred Pipe" and its powers and to make sure that it wasn't being used to overthrow the government through espionage or sabotage. So I told them that the spirit was going to show them what investigation was really about.

So we sang a song, and that spirit of the stone-people came in. We put all those stones in a big circle and put gold on top of it and called it the Capitol. So those stones that building is made of, they know everything that goes on in there. They hear those secret meetings. So those stone-people went to a vault there that contained secret papers and brought one of those documents into our lodge. You could hear that paper rattle inside the lodge.

Normally, paper wouldn't sound like that because it is so wet in there that it would just get limp from all the moisture.

So we opened the door to read that piece of paper. It gave instructions that all the Indian land was to be taken. No matter how you get it, get it. If necessary, kill them to get it. That was the secret document they brought in.

Well, these guys were really surprised. They started saying that they didn't know about that document. They had never read it. They were only citizens that had been hired to do a job. They had their orders that they had to carry out because that was their bread and butter. So they learned that we Earth People can know what goes on behind closed doors.

When they came out of the lodge they still carried that little shadow of doubt in their minds. So the spirit had another lesson ready for them. I said, "The spirit told me that you guys brought guns here. You're undercover, so you have that permission to carry those guns. But we don't bring guns to the stone-people-lodge. It is sacred here. We don't bring our weapons to pray with. They don't have that power here. This is the home of the fire, so the spirits have that power in their hands. So to show you that power, they said you could take your gun, point it at me, and pull the trigger. They will stop that fire."

Because that shadow of a doubt was still there, those guys were too scared to do that. They trusted those guns more than the spirit. They thought the spirit was a liar. Maybe they just thought I was a liar. So I asked to see one of those guns. This guy gave me his gun. I pointed it up in the air and pulled the trigger. It just went "click." That's all. Then their eyes got big. So they saw that power, and they knew it was real. But the spirit told us in the lodge that those two were not going to make that report to their superiors about our powers.

So we were told by the old people about the sacredness of this lodge. You start very simple. The most simple way is the best. So every step you walk to the lodge is a prayer. From there you walk off, and every step you take is a prayer. The old people told us this. So every step you take is a prayer. But it seems like some people are in the wrong step. If you take a wrong step, then you are in the wrong all your life. If you take a right step, then you'll be in the right the rest of your life. So the right step is from this lodge. So wherever you stop, always stop at this lodge. You come here to renew and rededicate yourself. You go from here for two or three months, then stop at that lodge.

So the old people say it this way. Before you even lift this foot and plant it, you have to look where you are going to plant it. That's always best. There are always obstacles in your path. You could step on pebbles, or you could stumble or kick and fall over. So it's best to lift this foot and place it in the stone-people-lodge. That is the best place to put your foot. It's the best place to stop. From there you go on for another two or three months.

So it's a place where you go to be purified. When you pray for people, you have to wipe yourself on the last round. Then all the contamination will go away. Whatever your intentions are, the spirits will add more power, more strength to it. So they give you that back. Good words and good thoughts will come out. Then you think something good, and you do something good. So they return you with that power built inside of you.

Now we come to the word *sweat-lodge.* That's just a nickname. Naturally, when we crawl in and hot rocks come in, we sweat. We perspire. So they call it a *sweat-house,* or *sauna*—you could call it that way, too. But the spirit told us that that term is not ours. He said, "I will tell you the truth: *Tunkan tipi.*" That's the real name—*tunkan tipi. Tun* means "birth," and *kan* means "age." The word *tipi* in the Lakota language means a "windbreaker" or "shelter." Even that four-legged that bores a hole into the ground, that is his tipi. And *tezi* means "stomach" or "womb." So this lodge is *tezi.* That's where the stone-people live. They contain all the elements that form the human structure. Then we put that fire back into those stone-people. So there's a fire. There's also a fire that lives in you. There's a spark in there. We call it soul or spirit.

When we crawl into that lodge, we crawl in on our hands and knees. So we're four-leggeds again. We get down there and crawl in. You have to be humble to crawl around on fours. So we crawl in in a humble way. Then we visit the stone-people. When we close that door to the lodge, we go back into our Mother's womb to be purified, see? So we go there and make offerings. Then we tell our little problems, and that blows away. So we contaminate that air. Then, when we open the door, all that contamination goes out. It expels out, and new, pure air comes in. The fresh oxygen comes in again. So we use oxygen and hydrogen together, see? When the door is closed, the temperature rises, and that expels all that poison out of our body. We open and close that door four times during the ceremony.

When we come to this lodge, we come here to paint those stone-people red. We say it that way in our language. We don't say we come here to heat up the rocks. There's also a powdered paint we use to paint them when a person goes on a vision quest or there is a healing ceremony. I told you about going to the Badlands to get that powdered paint. So we know how to find those powdered paints.

Now, like I prayed because my dad was sick. So the spirit came in, and I prayed with those powdered paints. Then the spirit took those powdered paints and said, "This is sacred." Then he drew a line over and across that rock pit in the lodge. So from there I walked across it, and my dad crossed it, and we came out alive. No scientist could ever do that. You could draw a line on a paper, but you can't draw a line over a rock pit with powder. But this spirit will draw a line with that powdered paint, and you will walk over it. So there are a lot of mysteries, sacred ways. I haven't really told you what they could do, because what I saw was even much greater. I don't think scientists will really understand, because it's by far a much deeper power. The scientist has to see it with his eyes first. He has to use a microscope or have a little picture of it, what it's shaped like. If it's not there, then it's nothing. So these powdered paints are just one mystery.

We couldn't be going there all the time to get those paints, because the Indians leased that land to the government, and, in turn, they used it for bombing practice. So they have to use that land to pound Grandmother. It's like using her for a punching bag. So we have to use substitutes for those paints. For example, we used those paints to color our tobacco ties. The old people used to make their prayer ties from pieces of buckskin that were painted with those powdered paints. Since we couldn't go there, my grandfather asked the spirits for permission to use a substitute. Because we are so pitiful, that request was granted. The spirit told him to use that cotton that grows here. They spin it into thread and then make it into materials. So we began to use that colored cotton cloth as a substitute. We cut that into little squares for our tobacco ties, prayer ties. We always try to use pure cotton cloth so we can be as close to natural as we can.

So it's hard for us to gather the materials we need. They are on the land, but that land is federal or state or private land. So you can't walk on these private lands. There's a *no trespass* there. If you go there and try to pick medicine, they will shoot at you. Sometimes they shoot us dead. Then the government comes and says, "Well, a dead Indian is a good one," like that. So it's really hard to go in any land. It used to be our land, but it's like they pulled the rug out from under our feet. So we are a people without a land and without a law. The spirit told us, "Not even one law was ever made for the Indian." So investigate that, because that is what the spirit told us. So every law that was made for Indians was made to go against us. So there never was a law made for Indians. So these things happened to us.

When we conduct a stone-people-lodge ceremony, someone has to sponsor that lodge. It takes time to sponsor a lodge. It's not like you just jump in and turn on the heat. It's not that way. You have to do it in a sacred way, then it's going to work for you. Each time we run a lodge there has to be a new set of robes and ties. You can't be using them over and over. When the lodge is over, we roll those prayer ties into a ball. Then you lay those robes together with the black robe on the bottom. You set that ball of ties in the middle and fold it all into a knot. When you are finished, the black robe will be on the outside of the bundle. Then you take this bundle up to a mountain or hill. You find a virgin spot where there are no tracks, where there's a lot of bushes or tall grasses. You tuck it in there or put it in the crouch of a tree or lift a rock and put it underneath. Then you say a prayer. "Grandfather, Grandmother, we thank you very much for the wind. We thank you very much. Here, take this." Then it will turn to earth. That material will turn to dirt again. You return, but that life will go. Once the spirit touches it, it is a life.

We've proven that. On one vision quest we used these big robes. They were one yard apiece. After you return from the vision quest, it is customary to leave the robes at the vision quest site for four days. So on the fourth day we went back there. Those robes had been torn to pieces and were lying scattered on the ground. Some robes were cut into strips and some were tied into knots. Two robes were missing. The lodge was upside down and all the legs were broken. The canvas lodge covers were torn and scattered all over. Even the tobacco ties had been cut. They had cut them with a sharp knife or maybe a razor blade. They were cut clean and all the tobacco was gone. Maybe they smoked it. Maybe they thought it had some kick in it. So my boys, they got really mad and started cursing. So I said, "Hey. Hey. Don't be saying those words here, because this place is *wakan.*"

So the next year we went back there. We gathered what was left and prayed there. Then we brought those remains back to the lodge and prayed there. We added more robes and bundled up the ones that had been desecrated. So we put some new robes over them. Then we took it back up to the mountain, looked around, and placed them there in a good spot.

The next year we went to that same place for vision quest. Two of my boys came there. When they were finished, I went there to pick them up. They asked, "Shall we take the robes down?" "No. I think we will go right away. At least for a day, or maybe this afternoon we'll come back." So we went back. After the ceremony, we ate. "Okay, we're going back there. So I'll come with you." When we went back up there, they were gone. "Oh, no. Not again. Not again."

So we prayed. So I told them to go into that hole, into that arbor. Go in there and see. So they went inside. Those robes were all there hanging inside. Those tobacco ties were hanging in there also. Even those torn ones were in there that we had buried, like the day we made them. So that was a mystery. So those robes and ties have a life. So there are a lot of things that we have to understand. You shouldn't worry, you should only trust the Great Spirit. But you have to believe it. In what you say, you have to humble yourself. You have to remember what you say. Lots of people say things they forget.

So one time we had a stone-people-lodge ceremony, and two people came in. Nobody knows where they came from because everybody was busy getting ready—undressing and lining up. These two people just came out of nowhere. They just happened to fall in line. They walked right in. Everybody crawled in and sat down. They sat in the back on the north and east sides of the lodge. During the prayer round when it came time for them to pray, each one of them talked or prayed for about forty-five minutes each. So they were talking there for about forty-five minutes each—an hour and a half! So it was really long.

When they finished, the spirit said, "Those two talked to me a long time. They were going so fast, I didn't hear what they were saying. There's a line drawn across this doorway. There's a line. When those two pass that line, they are going to forget me." That's what he said.

After the ceremony, those two left. So people started asking who they were. They asked the person who was standing behind them in the line, "Did you know them?"

"No, I didn't know them."

So we asked the guy who was standing in front of them.

"No. They just fell into line and followed me in. I don't know them. I don't know where they came from. I never saw them before."

So up to this time we don't know who they were or where they came from. So we have all kinds of experiences. All kinds.

One time we had a stone-people-lodge, and my cousin was pouring water [leading the ceremony]. I said, "Cousin, do you want me to sit across the door from you?" That way we help each other. When I sing, he pours water for me. When he sings, I pray or pour the water. So we help each other that way.

So he started praying. Then the prayer started going around to the other people inside. The way he runs the lodge, he keeps the door closed during the prayers. That's the original way. Some people can't stand it that way, because by the time it gets to the end of all the prayers, you're getting hotter and hotter. The way he does it, when a person finishes praying he pours water for them, and they bless themselves with the steam. So it gets hotter and hotter in there. So the longer you pray, the hotter it gets. So he went around, and about half way around some of the people in there started screaming, "Open the back window. Open the door." Like that. The others started screaming, *"Mitakuye oyasin. Mitakuye oyasin."* That's Lakota for "all my relations." When they say that in the stone-people-lodge, that means to open the door. So either my cousin or I will tell the fireman outside the lodge to open the door.

But these other people had to pray first. So I said, "Pray. Pray." Then a girl sitting back there said, "All my children." She forgot how to say it. So another person yells out, "All my relations." So my cousin said, "Oh, open the door for them." Then we continued. Then we closed the door again.

There was a white girl in there also. She was the wife of my adopted brother. So my cousin asks, "Who's that girl? That white girl, I'm going to pray for her. At least mention her first name." That's his way. He wants to honor every division. Those robes we use represent the four divisions—the black, red, yellow, and white nations. So he wants to honor her that way.

Well, since she is our sister-in-law, in a joking way we call her "Sugar." In Lakota we use the word *chahanpi* for sugar. But that word doesn't really identify sugar. *Cha* means "wood" or "tree," and *hanpi* means "the tree sap." That identifies maple sugar. When you evaporate the water from that sap, there is just syrup. So that is sweet. The same applies to sugar beets and sugar cane. So there are a lot of sweets out there.

So my cousin said that we were going to tease her and call her *Chahanpi* instead of "Sugar." So we closed that door and the spirit came in. Then my cousin prayed, "Tunkashila, bless that white girl. My cousin said her name was *Chahanpi.*" Then the spirit said, "We like that name. So that will be her name." So the spirit approved and called her *Chahanpi.* So then I translated that for my white brother. *Cha* is a tree, and *hanpi* is the sap or juice. So she said, "Oh, that's good. I'm really glad. At least I have an Indian name." So we call her "Wood Juice," but the spirits approved that name. So it's really funny. "Wood Juice," that's really a funny name.

One time I got a call to do a stone-people-lodge in Washington, D.C. They wanted us to come there and instruct them in what the stone-people-lodge was all about. So we went there. We flew in and went to a big office there. The highest educated people, the highest paid professionals were there. They all wore suits, white shirts, neckties, and each one of them was carrying a little pad with them. All the biggies were there—"Mr. President," "Mr. Chairman," and like that, you know. Then there were the advisers—secretary, treasurers, more directors, and all this stuff, and I don't understand this stuff. Anyway, finally we got everything and everybody together. So now, how are we going to have this stone-people-lodge?

So I began to explain it. Well, first you have to have a Chanunpa. Then there's red wool, 100 percent virgin wool, eagle feather and plume, and conch shell. Right away it was, "Well, we can't have that. I don't think we can get an eagle feather." It was like that. So they started checking things off. "Oh, we might get a piece of 100 percent red wool." So one person goes to a closet and pulls out a wool jacket. "Will this do?" So here are these highly educated people, and they bring in something that they are going to throw in the trash or give to the Salvation Army. They think that will be all right for the spirit. They think that way, but they are educated. So I have to tell them that they have to have a new one, because they are not really educated in the sacred ways.

Then we went on. You have to have cotton, 100 percent cotton cloth. You have to have that in six colors—black, red, yellow, white, blue, and green. Then you have to have cotton string, twelve-gauge string, parcel-post string. But they don't know what that is, so they brought some real hard twisting twine. So they don't know what number-twelve cotton string is. Then Bull Durham for the prayer ties. The American Tobacco Company makes that. So I have to explain all of this to these big government people. They are all well educated. They read books about Indians and accumulate all this information.

It was kind of scary there. They call it the Bureau of Indian Affairs. They had all these advertisements, flyers, and pictures hanging there. Then there were newspapers, magazines, and books there. They have all the volumes on Indians. So these people were experts, and they were well educated. So they all came and wanted to know if we were going to have a stone-people-lodge. So I kept going on. They have to have water, corn, berries, and meat. "Okay." They wrote it down. So then they started dividing it all up. "Okay, who wants to take care of the food?" Then the secretary writes it all down, who is going to get what, what's your phone number, and like that. So every time I mention something, somebody takes that. "What else?" Well, you need a bucket, a dipper, some spring water, and deer antler prongs to lift the stone-people. Then we have to have saplings for the lodge frame and the covers. You need canvas to cover the lodge, or you could use bedspreads or blankets, or we could stop at a lumber yard and get some number-six black plastic.

So they kept writing it all down. "Okay, no problem. Who's going to take it? You. Okay."

So everybody was taking part. Everybody went to work. Some were picking up the telephone and calling.

"Okay, that's taken care of."

"No. I don't care. I took care of the things I was suppose to get. I got mine. So no problem."

So everybody kept checking and itemizing that list. Finally, they got it all together. So let's go over there.

So on the way we have to stop to pick up some groceries. Then we stop for lunch. Then we go check into a motel, and from there we go up the mountain. It was a national forest. So everybody was there. The whole bureau was there. There are fifteen departments, and each head of each department was there. So they had to put their heads all together. So when we got up to the mountain the park manager was there. He said, "Well, you have to park here." So there is one van that will take all our materials up there, but the rest have to walk up the trail. So we walked up there. Well, these people sit in the office all day, so it was really hard for them to walk up that mountain wearing full suits. We got a little over half way up when that guy that ordered [us to walk], he played out. "Well, this being the first time, I think we had better go back and drive our cars up." Okay. So everybody started coming down. Then everybody drove up.

When we got there that place was full of weeds. So we had to clear all that out before we could build the lodge. Then I marked the lodge, the fireplace, and the altar.

Then I said, "So, where are the saplings?"

This guy spoke up, "Well, I'm sorry . . . ah . . . I went to that forest. I saw some real small, you know, long trees that I thought we could use. So I stopped there. Then this national park guy came and told me that we are not supposed to cut the trees. So I went back, and I called my friend. So my friend had some green lumber. He had some oak two-by-fours and two-by-sixes, so he could make strips like laths. They are still green, so he said they would bend. So I ordered some. I brought a whole bunch of them in case some of them break."

So he had brought the whole bunch up there on the top of his van. So I marked where the door went, and then I marked sixteen holes for the frame pieces. By that time my sister arrived, so I had to leave them with the proper instructions. Each hole is about eight inches deep and [the bottom] slants towards the center of the lodge. That way, when you stick the frame pieces in the ground and bend them [together], the ends don't fly out of those holes. So you put the sticks into the ground and bend them [over toward the center] and tie them together. There is a certain way you do that. When you are finished there is a square formed [by the frame] directly over the center pit of the lodge. Then you tie a hoop all the way around [the side] to keep the upright sticks in place. While I was explaining all of this, one guy was standing there writing this all down. He even drew a little sketch of the lodge.

So I left with my sister. We got back that afternoon. It was a big mess. Some sticks were sticking way out there, and that lodge was really high. Normally, it's about three feet high on the inside, but here when I walked into it I couldn't reach the top. One guy already said, "Something tells me that we're not doing this right. When Black Elk comes back here and sees this, you know, I think he is going to tear it down." He was right. Some of those pieces were only about an inch into the ground. So the whole lodge needed to be redone. They were all well-educated people, but they did the sloppiest job I've ever seen. I think my five-year-old grandchild could have done a better job than that.

So everybody went home. The next day they all came back up there. This time they wore work overalls and blue jeans. So they got rid of those fancy clothes and dressed like me. It took them all morning to dig out the holes. Then that afternoon I began to place in the pieces and bend them over. We broke a lot of them. We just barely had enough pieces to finish. All the rest were broken up. Then I asked for the canvas cover. They brought out a little piece. It was only about five or six feet long, so it didn't even cover the whole lodge. It was a canvas, but you could see through it like a cheesecloth. So we needed that black plastic. Well, this guy had gone to get it, but it was Saturday so that store was closed. So instead, he brought up enough [rolls of] black shingle paper to cover 250 square feet. So we gave that a try, but those strips kept sliding off that dome. So we tried fastening them together with little sticks, because we didn't have any way to glue them together.

When I looked inside, there were a lot of holes. So now we have to use anything we can get our hands on. So we bring out blankets, sleeping bags, jackets, towels, and like that. We just barely got it closed up. Then we had to tie string all the way around to keep those things [strips of shingle paper] from sliding off. It looked pretty funny.

Then it was time to start cleaning up and start the fire for the rocks. "Where's the saw? Where's the wood?" So then they brought little sticks. They picked up little skinny branches and put them in a big pile. I looked at it and said, "What is this? Is this a crow's nest?" I was teasing them that way. So I had to explain to them what "wood" was. "Wood" meant logs. So I needed logs that were four or five feet long. Well, this one guy was supposed to bring the wood and stones. So it's in his van. "Well, why don't you bring it on over?"

So he came over there carrying a paper box. Well, where's the wood? Well, he's bringing it in a paper box. Then the rocks. He was to bring thirty-six rocks, but the ones he brought were only about three inches in diameter, and we needed rocks that are about the size of your head. So I teased him also. "What did you plan to do here? Were you going to have a wiener roast or toast marshmallows? Looks like you were going to have a quick one at that."

So we go on. "Okay, bring out that saw." Well, it's a little key saw. Anyway, I have to turn their heads around, and I have four boys cutting big logs. Boy, they were really going. They just barely cut four. The others, I had them all over picking up wood. Some of it they broke up and put in a big pile. Other pieces they couldn't break, so they set them in another pile. Then I had to march them all the way down to the river bed to pick up rocks. So then they started carrying those stones back up there. Some of them would pick up three or four, then go a little way, then have to put one down. Then carry two, then put another one down. That was too much for them. None of them, not even one made it halfway back. So they had to go get a truck to haul those thirty-six rocks up there.

Then I set those stones over the logs. Then I stacked all those little and big pieces of wood in there tight. Then I put up the stone-people-lodge altar. "Okay, who's going to present the Chanunpa?" So my sister was there, and she wanted to present the Chanunpa on the behalf of all those BIA people there. So we filled the Chanunpa. Then we lit the fire. The fire started.

"Okay, where's the sacred food?"

Someone said, "Oh, no problem. It's over there in one of those little paper sacks."

So we go over. Now we're going to need a can opener. So we started to open those cans. They brought water from the faucet up there in a thermos bottle. So we poured that into one of those bowls. Then we poured in that can of blueberries and corn and corned beef. Well, here again these are supposed to be the highest educated and highest paid people, and they brought a can of corn, a can of fruit, and a can of corned beef.

Anyway, I sat there for a moment. "Okay, where's the bucket and where's the dipper?" You know those little plastic buckets that kids play in the sand with? That's what they brought up there. And for the dipper, there was this little soup dipper in there. So I had to tell them, "Oh, no. That's not it. That's nothing. That one you're going to have to throw away." By that time those guys were really getting on my nerves. They finally got to me. There's a whole bunch of them, and everybody's got questions. "What's this?" "Where does this go?" "Shall I put this here or over here?" So I was having one heck of a time.

So we drove down there and went to a hardware store. So it's closed. Then we call this guy on the phone and ask him to come down and open up that store for us. So he does that. I marched in and picked out a fourteen-quart bucket and a dipper. "Okay, this is a bucket, and this is a dipper." So I bought some extra dippers. Also we had to get some water containers—five gallons, turn-upside-down-and-drink—them kind. They got five of those. Then we drove back up the mountain. By now it's too late, so we have to wait another day.

Finally, it's that morning, so everybody is supposed to get up there early. The day before, everybody registered with one man, and he is supposed to ring their phone to wake them up. Everybody's supposed to put on warm jackets and heavy shoes, because it's cold up there. So everybody came there, and some were wearing blankets, and we went up there to that lodge.

There I filled the Chanunpa, and the daybreak was coming. When I filled the Chanunpa my wife, Grace, played the drum and sang the pipe-filling song. Then we all heard an *eagle-bone whistle.*

"What's that?"

"Where did that come from?"

"Did you hear that?"

"I think it came from back there."

"No. It came from that direction."

"No. I swear it came from that direction."

"No. It came from right behind me."

"No. It came on this side."

So that whistle came there from all directions. Just one whistle, but nobody knew what direction that whistle came from. Then I started to sing with that Chanunpa. I sang that offering, dedication song. Here these birds came, and a man appeared. So everybody could see him. He just came out of the woods and stood there. Those birds called to each other. They talked. So this was the first time they heard these birds talk—that whistling and chirping above us. Then you could hear this little gourd rattle, right there in the green. "Is that a snake? Is that a rattlesnake?" Like that. So we prayed. Then I offered tobacco to Tunkashila, Grandmother, the Four Winds, to the Eagle Nation, and back down to the stone-people. Then we lit that fire. So it was going.

After that, we passed that smoke around. Finished. Then we waited for those stones to turn red.

"Okay, it's time. Everybody get ready to go in." So we crawled in there, and the spirit came in and sat down. So he said, "These people have one foot over here and one foot over there." That's what he said. So they had one foot in that lodge and one foot in the government over there. Anyway, I'm to run a lodge like that with these fifteen department heads from the BIA, others from the national forest department and the road department and like that.

So after we came out, that forest service guy was crying. He said, "I'm so ashamed and embarrassed. Why do I have to deny Tunkashila? I thought he created all of this. Why do I have to be a stranger? Why do we have to use throw-away boards [scraps] and things like that? We should give the best we can!" Then those road guys spoke up. "This year we are going to blacktop this road up here. I think we should clean up this place so it will be presentable. We'll bring the best robes and lodge covers here. And the next time we come here, we are going to bring real spring water. We'll have that spring water here. We'll bring a big tank. We'll bring the best foods here. We'll bring fresh fruit, and for that meat, we'll get some buffalo and bring here." They were all talking that way. So everything got turned around. So that was my lodge in Washington, D.C. It was really tough to educate those educated people.

So let's talk about technology. We tried to talk to those nuclear physicists, and they wanted to bring this little gadget called radar over here. They wanted to throw a radar on the stone-people-lodge. So I said, "Sure. Bring it over. Technology and science began here. We kept the original technology and science, so bring it on over." So they wanted to see that spirit on there. They wanted to know if he comes in from the top or sides or from underneath.

So they have to string that big cable down there to the lodge and clear out those trees so they can get their equipment in there. So that took a lot of work and money, but they did it. So these guys, they are the ones that invented that radar, so they wanted to see what was going to happen. So they were behind this little screen, and we crawled in. But one scientist, he was the boss, he crawled in there with us and sat in the back behind that pit. Then they brought in the stone-people and the Chanunpa and robes, and everything was there. So we closed the door, and that black light came in, and the fire was there. So we have bright light and black light. When that black light comes in, then that spirit comes in, see?

So this scientist in there, he relies only on his naked eyes to see. We have two pairs of eyes, but we don't see two circles. We see one circle. But behind that there is another eye, called mind's eye. They are like two (pair of) lenses that you focus. Now normally, if you want to see those little molecules, genes, or organics you need the aid of a microscope or laser beam. But here in this lodge, the power was there, and it opened his mind's eye. It was the first time that had ever happened to him. Now he could see all those molecules, genes, and organics. He could smell and taste and feel everything. You can even close those front naked eyes, but you'll still see them with that mind's eye. So this black light is sacred.

So now he could see these little guys. He could see them move around. So he didn't need a microscope, he just needed that black light. So he took a glimpse at it. He got just an inkling of it. He could see those lights. He could see those gourds and the whistle. And inside that whistle, he could hear those voices. That is science. So when that spirit comes in, he talks through that whistle. We call it *jo jo.* That means "whistle talk." Or through that gourd, like a baby rattle, he talks. He talks inside. So if you come in there, all you're going to hear is a whistle and a gourd. But when the medicine man comes in and takes this plant and puts it into your ear, then you are going to hear them like we are talking. So there is a telepathic wave of intelligence that comes in. So this happened to this scientist.

So now he saw, and now he knows. Now he knows what we've been missing all the time. What we miss is the spirit. So it was really good that that happened to him. So he thanked me, and I thanked him. We both thanked each other. So now he goes outside. Then he tries to explain to these other guys what he saw inside. But these people, it's like "no comprehendo." They want to have what they call technological figures on a piece of paper. They've got to have proof before they accept it. But he doesn't have any paper to prove to them, so they reject him. So he's the head of that department, so they should listen to him. But instead, they put him down. They won't believe. So instead of accepting him, they labeled it "twentieth-century witchcraft." So here is the scientist that developed this radar. He blueprinted it. The highest technology. So it's kind of hard. It's bad enough to be called a dumb Indian, but to call their own highest intelligence man a witchcraft, that's kind of sad.

Anyway, he got mad. "Okay, what did you guys see on the radar screen?"

So they said, "Well, we saw a bunch of flickering lights, assorted flickering lights. We saw waving lights. We saw broad lines come right through the screen." So they never heard, smelled, tasted, or felt anything. All they saw were lights.

So he asked, "Okay. How do you interpret that? How do you translate what you saw on the screen?"

So they said, "Well, stand by, we have an audio problem. We have network difficulties."

So it was like a joke. And these were the highest educated people assembled there. But over here we don't have any audio or network difficulty inside the stone-people-lodge, because Tunkashila is there. And our mind's eye is open, and that's communication, see, because Tunkashila created the mind. But we kind of blanked out. Our mind's eye is blank, so we rely just on our naked eyes. So we cut off the hearing. So we lost that communication.

At least it was a breakthrough. I could say we cracked this nutshell. At least we had one scientist inside who saw and heard the spirit. Those other people, they didn't really know what they saw. They only saw flickering lights and waving lights or broad lights on the screen. So that was my experience with the nuclear physicists. I was thankful that Tunkashila blessed me for it. I am thankful that there are people concerned enough to come this way and question these powers.

One time we were at a *longhouse*. The longhouse people were there. We went in, and they had gourds there. Big gourds. They had them in a pasteboard box. The people that were there were sitting on a platform. There were about seven or eight singers sitting there, and they shook those gourds. There was a big drum there also, about a five-gallon water drum. It was a wine keg, wooden wine keg. They cut the top off, poured water inside, and stretched a skin over it. Then they placed Bull Durham four times, signifying the Four Directions. One guy played that drum. My dad performed the ceremony. So we asked to borrow one of those gourds. "Sure. It would be an honor. Here, take this one." So my dad had his altar there. So we placed that gourd on the altar on the ground.

Then they sang four songs. They rolled that drum and danced to it. When I sang that spirit came in and picked up that gourd [from the altar]. Then it hit that gourd really hard on the ground, like he was using both hands. There was a loud boom, and a flash of lightning came out. That gourd started bouncing around on the ground—tap, tap, tap—hitting hard like that. Each time it hit, a flash of lightning would come out. If you hit an ordinary gourd on the ground that hard, it would break to pieces. But this gourd started going around those tobacco ties lying all around the altar on the ground. It went all the way around.

So those longhouse people sitting there were trying to figure out how that gourd did that. They imagined that I was on my hands and knees crawling all the way around. When it came back, it started bouncing around about three feet off the ground. So now I stood up and started shaking that gourd, going all the way around the altar. Now, on the third round, that gourd is about seven feet in the air. So now I'm holding the gourd over my head and going around. Then the fourth round. Now you see that gourd hitting the ceiling. "Oh, oh. How could he get up there? That ceiling is much higher than he could reach." So that fourth round alleviated all their doubts. It just moved that doubt out. Like they thought I was the one doing it, but it was the spirit. So the spirit gradually removed that doubt.

So we have gourds. Then the spirits come in, and they pick it up. They shake that gourd. Like I said, it sounds like a baby rattle, but inside they talk. Then I translate for them because I can hear that talk on the inside. So when that medicine man puts that medicine in your ear, you're going to hear that talk. You could hear and understand any language. You don't have to speak it to understand it. Even if they change languages, they'll change you real quick so you could understand it or even speak it.

So that spirit told us in the longhouse about those sacred bundles the longhouse people had hanging in there. One bundle had a Chanunpa in it, one had a whistle, and one had a medicine in it. That medicine in there could cure cancer. But right there they had a whole family that was dying of cancer. Every time they went into the hospital they got the full treatment. They would cut off a little piece, then they would go back, and they would take another piece. But the cancer is still going. So they go in and take another piece. Pretty soon they are all chopped up and nothing is left. So that medicine was sitting right there in front of them. But they were all tied up in Christianity and had been brought up educated. So they didn't know what was in those bundles. They just knew they were sacred bundles, so they left them hanging there in the longhouse for years. But we came there, and the spirit told us what was in there. So they have to learn how to use that medicine to treat the cancer. So I thought I'd tell you that.

Part 2

THE SACRED
MYSTERY POWERS

CHAPTER 6

Spirit Powers

Through this Sacred Pipe we go up to the mountain to the stone-people-lodge. From that *tunkan tipi* we go back to our Mother's womb. We go back to our birth to be purified. When you come out, that mountain is sacred, and this whole world is an altar. So you stand on top of this mountain, and from there you send a voice to Tunkashila.

So there is an electrical power that goes around this rock [Earth]. I think they call it gravitation or gravitation law. When you go through that, there's weightlessness. It's the same way when you go from the knowledge into the wisdom, there's weightlessness. But man cannot live up there [in outer space] forever. He has to pack some air up there. But through this Chanunpa, the spirits will take you there. Those star-people will take you there and let you stand there. They'll let you see, and you will be breathing. So we don't have to pack a space suit or a bottle of oxygen to go there. You don't have to run back when your air runs out. It's not that way in the power of Tunkashila.

So the spirit was here three nights ago. He said that there would be a time that they are going to give me the privilege to unbundle that main Chanunpa [White Buffalo-Calf Maiden Pipe], that first one. And he said, "I'm a spirit. Tunkashila sent me here. I'm a spirit. Tunkashila sent me here. And there are four holes in that sun, and inside that sun there is a land. No one is to touch that fire [nuclear energy]. That same fire was placed here, and man was not to touch it, because it's sacred. But when man discovered that fire, he made a destructive tool with it, so man will destroy himself."

So we took that sacred fire. We say that the knowledge [which comes from Grandmother, the Earth] is a power. There is a Tree of Knowledge and a Tree of Life. So from that drop of knowledge we made guns, and we call that a power. Now they demand everything at gun point. So man has threatened the whole world, but I think that threat is a crime. But if you understand the laws, if you want to be a lawyer, you are going to discover that any-body who has sense enough to resist that threat, they're called terrorists.

So it was really something that the spirit came and told us that. So we say *taku wakan.* That means "something almighty" or "something powerful." When you look up, you see a huge blue robe, and there are four holes in that blue robe. So there is a huge power that wears that immense blue robe, and that is the life. Now the scientist are looking around out there for the water and the green. They are looking around for that life out there. So they send those little gadgets out there to orbit around. I don't know how many miles an hour they are going, but it takes seven, eight, or nine months to reach one of those star-people. Then they fly by and take those pictures.

But in Tunkashila, there is no time. Everything moves in the blink of an eye. It's as fast as thought. So there is no speed there. There's no time in between. So I want to tell you why there are four holes in that blue. We have a permanent red stone man that is going around, and his home is *payamini pa.* You call it Halley's Comet, but that's just a nickname. So I don't think the scientists understand that. Even if I stood there before them and told them that the home of Halley was *payamini pa,* I don't think they would understand that. But that's where this stone man came from. That's his home.

Maybe I should be teaching astronomy. Those scientists, they put bears and dogs and rabbits and stuff like that up there. Like they call some of them the "Little Dipper." But we don't call them bears or rabbits or draw a man up there holding a big sword and a shield. It's not that way. We don't name them that way, because each one has a language of their own. So there are a lot of people who don't know. There's a time when you could see a woman standing there with a Chanunpa. We know when that time is. So there are times they come and times that they go back. So they're here.

So when I went to vision quest, that disk came from above. The scientists call that a UFO—unidentified flying object—but that's a joke, see? Because they are not trained; they lost contact with the wisdom, knowledge, power, and gift. So they have to see everything first with their naked eye. They have to catch one first. They have to shoot it down and then see what all it is made of, how it was shaped and formed. But their intention is wrong, so somebody is misleading those scientists that way.

So that disk landed on top of me. It was concave, and there was another one on top of that. It was silent, but it lit and luminesced the whole place. It was dark, but those trees in front of me were luminesced like neon lights. Even the sacred robes there were luminesced, and those tobacco ties lying there lit up like little light bulbs. Then these little people came, but each little group spoke a different language. They could read minds, and I could read their minds. I could read them. So there was a silent communication. You could read it silent, like when you read silent symbols in a book. So we were able to communicate.

They are human, so I welcomed them. I said, "Welcome. Welcome. Hi, UFO's." They laughed at that, because they knew I was joking with them. So when you call them UFO, it's like saying they are foreign or unknown. So they thought that was a funny joke, so they laughed, because they are human, too. They liked that one. But the biggest joke is on those scientists, because they lost contact with those star-nation-people. When they see one of those little objects, they call it a UFO. They also have scientists who are hired to cover up the truth about those UFO's. They make up false explanations, like it was just some gas coming out of a lake or like that. But this one scientist, he told the truth, so they fired him from that job.

Someone even wrote about those UFO's in the Bible. Elijah went up into the clouds in a fire wagon. I didn't write that. So we know about that. We have UFO-people land here. We have star-people. The morning star comes and visits us. He comes when everything is asleep. So those of us who are up on time, you know, holding the Chanunpa, standing there to greet him, he comes. When he comes, you could see him coming. There is a sound with that. It sounds like the wind rushing. When he appears, he's like us. He talks. Then he goes. So a lot of people don't know about this way. But I learned this, and I saw it. I grew up with it.

When I used to get up, the first thing I would do is build a little fire for my grandmother. Then I would go out and get some water in a lard bucket. Grandpa would sit there and wait for that morning star, that *anpo wie*. Then he would go outside. He would hold up his arms and pray. It was beautiful. That star would dim and brighten, like in a fog. Then it would swirl back and forth and go back up. Then it would come back down or go sideways, stop, and shoot back up. Oh, it was so beautiful! So every day we would greet the morning star that way. My grandfather told me that when you held your arms up to pray there, it was like touching the face of Tunkashila. But a lot of people don't know about this.

Anyway, those little people laughed when I called them UFO's. But the one that stood in front of them, he was dead serious. He never cracked a smile. It seemed to me, he never even blinked his eyes. I got scared looking at his face and eyes. It gave me a spooky feeling. I had goose pimples down my arms and back and down to my legs. I felt like a little screen, like he could see right through me. It felt like a radar was going right through me. Then I started looking into his eyes. It was like a knothole. You know, if you have a pine board and a knot falls out, then there is a hole there. You only see a hole. But if you go close to that hole, you could see a vast area through that hole. That is the way I saw it in his eyes. So when I started looking into his eyes, it was like a little color TV. I could see a vast area back there. I could see everything in the universe through his eyes.

What I saw in there scared me. I saw these jets in there flying in formation, and I could hear them. Then a light came on, and they simply evaporated. They were gone. Then I saw steel tanks in there. When that light came on, they disappeared. They sizzled and bubbled, like when you pour water on a hot grill. So I got scared. So where is our military power going to stand when that power comes? They are no match. Everything will just evaporate. So there is no way of matching Tunkashila's creation. It's impossible to challenge the star-nation-people. It is impossible. So I learned something from those little people.

So I know about those spirit powers. There are rules for those powers. If you come to a ceremony with a tape recorder, there are rules for that. During the pipe-filling, that tape recorder should be turned off. You can play it before that or after that. If you want to take that recorder into an *altar ceremony,* you have to ask permission first in the stone-people-lodge. Then, before you go into the altar ceremony, you have to first wipe that recorder with sage. When you take it in, you have to leave a little piece of sage on top of it.

One time I took a tape recorder into an altar ceremony. I had a big, old tape recorder. It had a seven-inch reel. It was a big one. It was really heavy. I requested that I be able to use that recorder. The spirits said that I could even play those sacred songs on it, and they would come in. So in the ceremony we used that recorder. When we played those songs, they came in. So if you record a ceremony, the next night, if you turn on that recorder and play it, those spirits will come in.

One time I was recording a ceremony with that tape recorder. A spirit came in. It said that someone had come to visit me. So I asked him if that spirit that came to visit me was my grandmother.

The spirit said, "Your grandmother went to your house. Now she's coming this way. Now she's standing by the door. Now do you want her in here?"

So I said, "Yes."

So right away the people in there started singing. Then here she came. My mother got really scared, because she was half Christian. She started yelling, "Cover those kid's faces! There's a ghost coming in! Pray. Cover your head with your jacket." But me, I wanted to see my grandmother. Why should I call my grandmother in and then cover my face? If I have to cover my face, why call her in in the first place?

Anyway, I forgot that my tape recorder was still on. When my grandmother came in, I could see her. So I talked to her, and she talked to me. Everybody in there could hear that. Then she left. Afterwards, when we played that tape, her voice was on there. You could hear her talking to me on that tape. So I have a proof that that can happen. I still have that tape, and you could hear her on it. But those people who made this tape recorder, they don't know how to really use it. So we record, then we play, then we pray, then we play, and that spirit comes in, and we record that voice.

But if you don't ask permission first, and also put sage on that recorder, then the spirits will come and bust it, or they'll erase everything on that tape. They could short it out, burn it, because they are electricity. We saw this happen. We had an altar ceremony where a bolt of lightning came in. It hit one wall and bounced across to the other side of the room. There was a window there that was opened just a little bit. That bolt went out that opening and fired across to the house next door. The people were sitting in there watching TV. That lightning went there and burned up that TV. It burned the fuse box and knocked out about half the lights in town. We saw that happen. So when those spirits come, they are electricity, and they could knock off anything.

So we use sage to protect against that. So now we have to put sage on the fuse box and like that. Also, we have to cover up all the glass things, like mirrors or TVs, or put sage on them. When those lights come in, they reflect off of that glass. If the spirit sees that, he will go over there and break that glass. If he sees that reflection, that glass will just fall apart. That's the reason we cover them. In order to save those things, we cover them or put sage on them. If we put sage on a lantern, then they won't touch it. They'll bless you. They'll help you. They respect you. They know it. They read that sage.

So the spirits, they could do anything. They could reveal what you have on your mind, or they could read your life, like reading the palm of your hand. They'll tell you where you came from.

They'll tell you what all you did—good thoughts, good words, good acts, bad deeds, or whatever. Even if you steal something, they'll tell it. They'll tell where you put it. They could tell anything. So you can't hide anything from them. If you killed somebody and buried them at the bottom of the ocean, they'll go and see. They'll tell where you put him. They'll even bring him right to the altar, too.

I have this doctor friend. In the Lakota way, I adopted him as my brother. So he started toying around with ESP [extrasensory perception] because he had money. He went to an ESP school. So he went there with one of his friends because they could buy anything they wanted. So he wanted me to go to that school. The introduction was only $1.50, the initiation fee was $3.50, the lessons were $7.00, and like that. Well, when you kept adding that up, pretty soon the first week was going to cost you $75.00. Then who was going to pay for food, transportation, and a roof over my head? That wasn't added on there.

Well, I couldn't go to that school because I didn't have that kind of money. But we do have a Chanunpa. So I said, "Why don't we ask the Chanunpa?" So we had a Chanunpa ceremony. When the spirit came in, he asked what we wanted. So I said, "Tunkashila, I want to learn how the reading and writing began." But I'm not educated. If I spoke good English, I would have said, "Tunkashila, I want to learn how to read and write." That would have been the proper way. But since I'm not educated in those ways, I said, "Tunkashila, I want to learn how the reading and writing began." Then the spirit said, "That's impossible. But since you asked for it, we're going to give it to you."

So we sang a song, and there was a bolt of lightning. Then a little tiny fire came out of that Chanunpa and began to scrawl on a piece of paper, "Your dad was here at 5:30 [P.M.]. They'll be back here at 7:30. They're over at your brother's place now. When they come back here, they're going to have an altar ceremony here tonight. So you'll fill your Chanunpa and help your dad. I'm your grandma."

So we started moving our stuff to clear out a little room— enough for thirty people. We put our couches and beds outside into the yard. We covered all the windows. We blocked them off with cut-up boxes and tape. At 7:30 a car honked, and Mom came into the house. So we gave her that piece of paper, and she read it.

She said, "Yeah, I'm scared of you because you might be sacred."

So I asked her, "Did you come here at 5:30?"

She answered, "Yeah, we came here, but you guys weren't home. We want to have an altar ceremony. The food is all cooked, and the prayer ties are all made. But you guys weren't here, so we came back to check again."

So I said, "What time is it?"

She said, "Well, it's 7:30."

So I invited them to come on in. I started displaying the altar [setting up for the ceremony]. They got on the phone and started calling the other people. Pretty soon, cars started arriving. People started coming in and sitting down. Thirty of us packed in there. When everything was ready, we turned out the lights and began. So I caught the ESP just like that. A dumb Indian like me was given that power.

So my brother, this doctor, found out that I got this ESP from the Chanunpa. I didn't have to go to school for months and months and keep paying all that money. I got it in just a flash of lightning. So he and his friend came over to visit me because they were spending all that money on ESP school, and they wanted to know if I really got the ESP. So when my brother came there with his friend, he said, "I want you to meet my friend. His name is George Baker." So he wrote that name, George Baker, down on a piece of paper and then handed it to me. He asked me to use the ESP to write something on there about his friend.

All right. So I took that pencil and placed it on the paper. Pretty soon it started going around in a circle. Then it took off and wrote, "George Baker is a fictitious name." So my own brother was testing me. He was trying to see if the power of this Chanunpa was real or if I really knew ESP. Then that pencil wrote, "This man's wife is pregnant. She is going to have a baby. It will be born on March eighth at ten o'clock in the morning. She is going to have a girl. She will name it after her mother and her husband's mother. So on the one side the mother is Silva, and on the other side the mother is Phyllis. So she will name that child Silva Phyllis."

So they got real interested because they hadn't told me that this guy's wife was pregnant. So that man decided that he was not going to show that paper to his wife. If it happened that way, then he would show it to her. So they put it away. Then, on March eighth, that guy got up at six o'clock, because he takes off early for work. So at six o'clock his wife is up cooking, and there's no labor. She was just like usual, you know. So he thought that maybe it was to be another time. "Well, this time Chief is wrong. He's wrong." He was thinking that way.

So he took off for work. When he got to work, he got a telephone call. "You'd better get back here. Your wife is in labor. The baby is coming." So he drove back home. He picked her up and took her to the hospital. One-half hour later she had a baby girl, right at ten o'clock. So he went back to work. That evening, at seven o'clock, he came to the hospital to visit his wife and child.

He asked, "Have you selected a name yet?"

She said, "Yes."

"Well, what is it?"

So she answers, "It's Silva Phyllis."

So I proved to them that I had those powers. So now they try to test me that way. Sometimes I refuse. Sometimes I give the wrong answers. Then they think, "Oh, he's false. He's just a dummy." That way I escape, because some of them are too serious. Sometimes, I will be quizzed if I keep on. So I don't do that ESP much any more.

But I still use the Chanunpa that way. We had an altar ceremony, and a Mandan man came there and prayed. His son was in Vietnam, and he hadn't heard from his son in six weeks. So he started worrying. He wanted to know if his son was alive or hurt or lying in the hospital. He didn't know what was going on. So we sang a song, and the spirit came in. He said he would go over there and find that boy. So we started singing again, and that spirit scout left. We kept singing that one song, and I believe it was the fourth time, last time, that he came back in. The spirit reported that he had found that man's son, but that the son was depressed. So the spirit decided to boost his morale. Then he told us that tomorrow that boy was going to leave Vietnam. He said, "Tomorrow, he will be between earth and sky, and tomorrow afternoon he will land on this island again. And tomorrow evening, next day same day evening, he's going to sit behind the altar." So that spirit was going to discharge him from the war.

So right away they started figuring out the time—that would be thirty-six hours away. So the countdown began. These people never called the War Department, never asked anyone, or did anything. They just started counting down the hours. Then the next day it happened just like the spirit said it would. That boy flew into Denver and told us what had happened to him. He said that yesterday an officer came around and held a roll call. They thought they were going to be sent to the front, but there was really no front because they were just all over the jungle there. Anyway, the officer called out his name and said, "Get ready. Pack up because you are going back to the States." The boy couldn't believe what he had just heard. He said, "What?" and the officer said, "I said get up. You're going back to the States."

So everybody started yelling, hugging each other, and dancing around. Still he had a bad feeling because the others were not going to come home. Anyway, they took him to the airport, and they all piled into an aircraft and took off. They landed in Seattle. Then they took another plane to where they went through processing. They got new clothes, adjusted their pay, and like that. From there, they went in all directions, and he flew into Denver. So he was back in Denver that afternoon, just like the spirit said he would be. That night we held an altar ceremony for him, and he was sitting behind the altar. Thirty-six hours later, and his mother and father were coming there with tears in their eyes.

I told him, "We used Fast last night. He's a scout. He does strange things, unbelievable things. He does them lightning fast. He's not a medicine man [he doesn't heal]. He's a scout; he's a detective; he's an investigator. So he does things lightning fast. He told us that he goes around the world six times in the blink of an eye. So in the universe, he hears and sees everything all at the same time. That's how quick he is. So this electricity spins around the world six times in the time equal to the blink of an eye. So in comparison to the spirit, we're really slow. Over here, our technology and science are far, far behind." So he was really happy to be home.

So those spirits could do anything. One time there were these two kids playing here in Denver. I think that was in 1984. So here these kids found two skulls lying there and took them home. When the father saw them, he decided to turn them over to the authorities. So they brought them to the university, and they identified them as a man and a child. But they didn't know who they were. I had a nephew working there, and they asked him if he had any idea how to identify those skulls. He told them that they could present a Chanunpa to a medicine man, and he would find out. Then somebody suggested that he talk to those big guys about that. So he talked to them and convinced them to try it.

So my nephew came to me and asked if I would help. I said, "Sure." So we went to this house, and they brought those skeletons there in a box. There was wall-to-wall carpeting there, and those archaeologists, geologists, and anthropologists were all sitting there. And there were us two dummies there. I was to translate. I was to interpret when the spirit came in, because I knew how to talk to them. So my cousin was running the ceremony, and he asked me to speak to the spirits and then speak to these guys sitting there, because he didn't speak English. So that was my job.

So we prayed, and the spirit came in. He asked, "What do you want?"

So I said, "There are two relatives here that were found. We want to know what language they speak, and how they ended their lives."

So we sang four songs—the Four Winds direction. So the powers of the Four Winds were sent to single out those two and bring them back to the altar. On the fourth song, they brought them in.

There was a man and a boy. They were father and son. They spoke Arapaho. They told us how they had ended their lives. They said that they had gone out buffalo hunting. On the way back to their tribe, a blizzard came. So they laid down in the snow. Then they got cold and went to sleep. They froze to death.

So we learned about those skulls that way. Now that is science. That is what those archaeologists, geologists, and anthropologists should be doing instead of leaving those bones lying around in the museums.

So it's really unbelievable what those spirits can do. Another time my brother was performing a ceremony, and I was helping him. The prayer went all the way around [each individual had prayed], and the spirit said, "Is there anything else that you people might want to say before we leave?" So my brother-in-law was lying there in the closet. All the room had been taken up, so he was lying in there on all those toys and basketballs and stuff. They threw a mattress in there on top of everything so he could lie in there. So we were packed in there like sardines. Some of those people had driven a long distance to be there.

Anyway, my brother-in-law said to me, "Brother-in-law, ask the spirits if they could fix that TV. I hurt my leg, so I can't work. So now I'm a baby sitter. All these people are doing harvest. Some are picking potatoes, corn, or doing gardening or beadwork. Everybody is working. But since I can't work, everybody leaves their kids here. So I'm a baby sitter. That's my job: baby sitter. But I can't keep those kids together. Only that little box is what keeps them together. So I went and bought a TV for thirty dollars, but it went out. So I called for a free TV estimate. So he drove out here, and he estimated it would cost one hundred dollars to fix it. He said that the picture tube was out and that some of the other tubes were weak. So if I were to spend that much money, I might as well buy another TV for maybe forty dollars. So I wondered if the spirit could fix it."

So that spirit said, "Yeah. Roll it out here. Bring it over here."

It was on rollers, so they rolled it out into the middle of the room.

Then the spirit said, "We are technology. We are scientists. We'll show you. We'll demonstrate that we have that power, too. We have that power."

So when we started singing, those gourds went over there. You could see lightning and—boom—like a little hammer here and there. You could hear a crash and crunch, like glass breaking. They were pounding all over. It was an old TV, so it had tubes.

Pretty soon you could see light in those tubes. They were carrying those tubes all around the room. Wires were disconnected, and they were disassembling the whole thing. They were carrying all these pieces on the inside around, and, at the same time, they were talking also. Like when you turn on the TV, you hear the sound. And you could see part of the pictures on the TV screen, so the TV could be recorded by the spirit.

So then they went back in, and they were all over again. There were sparks here and sparks there, and sometimes you would see little blue streaks—shooooo—like welding. Inside that picture tube you could see a man dancing, and you could hear the music. But that TV wasn't plugged in. And they were talking inside that tube. Then they stopped. And the leader said, "Well, we're finished. After we depart from here, you are going to eat. You are going to smoke, drink water, and eat here. While you are eating, you could plug in the TV and watch it."

So after four songs, they departed. Then we turned on the lights. We lit the Chanunpa and passed it around for everyone to smoke. Then we passed around the water and sacred foods. Then somebody said, "Hey, plug in that TV. We're going to watch it." So we plugged it in, turned it on, and here it came. So I think they could fix anything.

I first saw this when I was real little. My grandpa and grandma bought a wood[-burning] cooking stove. They had to order it because they didn't have those kind of stores on the reservation. So the grocery store owner brought it out there in a Model-A pickup. It was a big, cast-iron stove. But on the way there, he bounced it around in that pickup and broke it. The leg was broken off, and it was cracked on the top and side. It was going to take maybe three or four months before they could replace it. So the owner said, "Well, okay, I'll let you have it for eight dollars." Well, our stove was rusted, and ashes fell in where you baked the bread, and it had no legs. We had filled up a washtub, and the stove was sitting on top of that. So my grandmother decided to take the broken stove. So we threw out the washtub and old stove and brought the new one in.

Then Grandma started making prayer ties for a puppy ceremony. You use a blue robe and ties for that ceremony. We painted red through the nose, ears, back, and down to the tail on the puppy.

"Now, puppy, we're going to need your help. You're going to go to West and bring those Thunder Spirits," Grandmother said.

So that puppy is the best friend to man, because he will give his life to help us. So while we were singing, Grandpa came back.

He asked, "What are you doing?"

So Grandma told him, "We're going to offer you a Chanunpa, and we're going to call the spirits. We're going to ask for help."

So we got everything ready—the food, ties, robes. Then she filled the Chanunpa and gave it to Grandpa. She presented it— held it out four times. He took it.

Then he said, "So this is health and help. We need help. So we are going to use this help that way. I bought this stove, but it's broke. So I'm going to have them fix it for me."

Grandma said, "Oh, good."

So we displayed that altar and called in the spirit. He said, "What do you want?"

So Grandma said, "I have tobacco ties and robes for you. I also have a puppy here. So I sent that puppy to bring you here for help."

Then the spirit asked, "So what is it that you want us to do?"

Grandma answered, "I bought a stove, but the end is broken. The top is broken, and the leg is broken."

Then Grandpa said, "Oh, start now. Sing four songs." We started singing, and those spirits were all over that stove. It sounded like they were using a sledge hammer on it—boom, bang. You could hear that sound of cast iron breaking, and pieces were flying all over the room. They beat it, and they stopped. Then they were gone.

So Grandpa said, "Let's turn on the lights and see. They were supposed to fix that stove, but we heard all those crashes. So let's see what they did."

So we turned on the lights, and, here, they had broken that stove to pieces. They had smashed it into a thousand pieces, and there was just a big heap lying there. So Grandma got real mad, just like a little kid. She yelled, "You come back in here. I offered this Chanunpa. I got some tobacco ties, robes, and a puppy here.

You behave yourself. I told you kids to fix this, now you damaged it. You broke it up. So now you fix it. You put it back." She was talking like that.

So we turned the lights out and sang a song. Those spirits came back in, and they were all over again. You could see those little lights all over—shoooo, shoooo—like little blue streaks. Then they stopped again. So there was a leader spirit. He's an interpreter. So we asked that leader what they had done.

He said, "Well, you asked them to fix it. So they have it all fixed." Then they went up and were sitting up there.

So Grandpa said, "Take the robes and ties. They're yours now. Take that little puppy, too."

So we started to pray and sang a song. Then that little puppy came in right through the wall. It came all the way around. It started jumping all over us, licking our faces, whimpering, and like that. He was really happy. Then he started barking at something. He was running in and out, but there was no door there, just a wall. Then he went to the altar and kept barking. The spirit said that he saw a sickness coming, so he started barking. He was chasing that sickness away. So he was doing more than just helping us fix that stove.

Then some *heyokas* [spirits that do everything backwards] came in. They started dancing and off beat. While they were dancing, they kept saying, "We're not here." That means they're here.

Then, "We're not going to help you." That means they're going to help.

"Don't smoke that Chanunpa." That meant smoke the Chanunpa.

"That Chanunpa is not *wakan.*" That's what they said. But that Chanunpa is *wakan,* so everything was backwards.

"Tomorrow all of you are going to be dead." So they say and do those things.

Then the interpreter for them said, "Now they say that I am supposed to talk to you straight. They helped you. You offered these ties and robes. They are thankful for that. They are thankful for that puppy." Then you could hear them eating that food. Finally, they finished.

"Oh, thank you. We're going to take off now."

So we sang four songs, and those little lights went up. Then, they were all gone.

"Okay, turn on the lights."

So we turned on the lights, and that stove was just perfect. There were no seams where it had been broken. The top, leg, everything was perfect. So we got a brand new stove for eight dollars. So the spirits could do anything. But if you use them, there is a certain order to it. They watch real carefully. First, they send in a scout, and he checks on everything. He even checks on what people have in their minds. If there is a shadow of a doubt someplace, that will cause a weakness. So, if a person puts up a ceremony, and one person comes there with a doubt, that will weaken the prayers of those people who are sincere. So one should not go there with doubts. Everybody should pray together, cheer along, root along. That brings the circle together. Everything is together. So these are the powers.

CHAPTER 7

Never Leave Room
for Doubts

One of the things the old people taught me about the spirits was to never have a doubt. When I talk about what the spirits can do, most people have that little shadow of doubt in their mind. So I'll tell you about that ceremony we were going to have. My uncles and aunts, they were all going to come to the ceremony. Some of my relatives live up on a little part of the highway coming down. They look down on our little log cabin and fireplace. So there were these four boys walking home from school. Two of them were my cousins. They go to St. Francis Mission School. They were walking down the highway, and they saw this fire at our cabin. "What's that fire for?" The other guy said, "Oh, they're having a *yuwipi* ceremony." That's a ceremony where the leader is tied up in a blanket and visited by the spirits.

"They're worshiping the devil." "They're possessed." They started talking like that. They believed it. But they got curious. "Hey, let's go there and see what is going on." So they came over there and sat down.

So while sitting there they started saying things like, "I hope God punishes them," and, "I hope the angel will come with the flaming sword and strike them dead." They were talking like that. So these four, educated guys believed like that.

Just then the stars are going this way and that way. And one of those stars comes shooting down—shoosh—and shoots into that cabin. So we're sitting inside the cabin, and there is this bang. That rock rolled right in. Then he started talking. So my grandpa was talking to that rock. And that rock talked to all of us.

"Glad to see you. Now I go. Now I go back."

Then he went—pang. Went right up, but there's no hole in that roof. It just went right through.

Now those guys were still sitting there saying, "I hope the angel of the Lord curses them and punishes them." They were still talking that way. But they saw that light come out, and they saw it go straight back up to the stars. So they got really going. "Now see, God's punished them." "Don't go over there because you might find them all lying there dead." "If you go there they might accuse you of killing them. So don't go there. Don't go near." They talked that way. But then shortly after that we all marched out of the cabin. So that really surprised them! Then they got more curious about that light.

So those guys that did that accusing came to our next ceremony. They still carried that shadow of a doubt, so the spirit came in and educated them. Two of them sat on one side of the room and the other two sat across from them on the other side of the room. For two of them, the altar was on their left side and the door was to their right. For the other two, the altar was on the right and the door to their left. Then we turned out the lights. Then that spirit came in. After the ceremony was over, we turned the lights back on, and the spirit had switched those [two pairs of] guys around in the room. The two boys on one side—the door was on their left when they came in, and now it was on their right. The other two boys were also now sitting on the opposite side of the room. So they tried to figure out who turned that house around. But this is just a log cabin with a dirt floor and a dirt roof. It only had one door. It was just a little square. So they started to ask, "What are you doing over there? How did you get over there?" That's the way the spirit educated them.

In that same ceremony we had a guy come from Manderson [South Dakota] up north. Before we started, he started saying, "I heard you Sioux played tricks. You take watches, rings, and billfolds." But no one said anything to him. So he just sat there. He was wearing a watch with one of those stretch bands on it. It didn't have a strap with a buckle on it. He wanted to make sure we didn't play tricks on him, so he held his hands together with his fingers interlocked together. He had rings on too. But nobody said anything to him. It was like he was just thinking aloud.

When that spirit came in, he saw that man in the pitch dark. He said, "There's a man here that has doubts against me. But I have the power, and I'm going to teach him so he'll never forget about it. They think they're educated, but I'm an educator, too. So I'll show them I'm an educator." That's what the spirit said, but nobody said, "Who? Who? Where? What's his name?" They just sat there in the darkness, in that black light.

So when they turned on the lights, that guy was still sitting there, and he still has his hands held together. My dad was at the altar. He was performing the ceremony. He looked down and said, "What is this?" And there was a wristwatch and rings there. A billfold was also lying there. So my dad asks, "Who does this belong to?" And this guy is still just sitting there. Then he notices that his wristwatch and rings are gone. So he starts feeling for his billfold, and his billfold is gone also. So he starts yelling, "Hey, that's mine! That's my money!" He takes that billfold and starts counting his money, but all the money is there. Then he takes a close look at his rings. They're not damaged, but they had slipped off his fingers. Oh, they probably didn't slip off, they probably just evaporated from there and reformed over here on the altar. That way the spirits could doctor his mind, and they could reform him. So those spirits they could do anything they want.

Years back we had this ceremony for my sister. My sister and brother-in-law, they're all Christian. So they never hardly come to the Chanunpa ceremony. They respect us and never speak against us, but at the same time they are sort of independent. They also believe in peyote ceremonies, but, again, they believe that Christianity is the way. They call it cross-fireplace [peyote ceremony], so they don't speak against the half-mooners [peyote ceremony]. They are always sort of neutral. They are good people. It's good to go to their place. They'll tell you, "Come sit down and have coffee. Make yourself at home." They say those kind of things. So it's good to go there and visit.

So they were working in Scotts Bluff [Nebraska]. On weekends they used to drive to a farm. They went there to buy eggs from a farmer. They paid twenty-five cents a dozen for them. They would buy those eggs, not by the carton, but by bucketsful. Then they would bring them home and put them in the freezer. A lot of people came, and they gave them eggs. So they were always passing eggs around.

One evening they were driving down that way on a gravel road. It was dark, and a car came from behind with its lights on. It was a little car. It got closer, so they slowed down for him to go around. Now when they slowed down that car came closer and started hitting their bumper. So they sped up. Then that car came close again. So my sister started saying, "Don't speed up. Don't speed up. They want us to go fast, and we might have a flat tire or you might lose control on this gravel."

My brother-in-law said, "Yeah, that's what I think, too, because when I slow down, they keep hitting the bumper."

Then he started feeling around in the car, and there was a single-barrel .22 rifle in there. He didn't know there was a gun in there.

"Hey! There is a gun in here! Well, I'm going to scare them."

So he stopped the car and opened the door. He got out and pulled that gun out. Then he leaned back against the [opened] car door with the gun in his hands. He held it up in both hands with the barrel pointed up [at a forty-five-degree angle]. But that little car had bright lights on them, so they couldn't see it. They couldn't see what kind of car it was, what color it was, what was the license plate, or anything.

After my brother-in-law got out, these two white boys [got out and] ducked down on the other side and came around in front of the [brother-in-law's] hood. But my sister saw them, so she started yelling, "There're two coming around behind you! Look out! Look out!" But it was too late. One kid grabbed his rifle, and the other one grabbed him by the neck and wrestled him to the ground. They took that rifle away and started kicking him and hitting him with that gun. So my sister jumped out of the car to help. Then two other guys jumped out of that little car, and they knocked my sister down. They started kicking her, but she managed to get away. She started running towards a farm there. The people that lived there were going someplace, so they had just happened to come outside. They heard a lot of screaming going on over there on the road, so they turned on their yard lights. So my sister ran over there to those lights.

That couple saw all this blood all over her, so they called the sheriff. By the time the sheriff got there those guys had jumped in their car and took off. So these two people that lived there and my sister, they couldn't see that car. All they knew was that it was a little car. They didn't know how many people there were either, because my sister had only seen the two guys that jumped my brother-in-law. But those other guys knocked her down, so maybe there were four of them. Anyway, they went over there with the sheriff, and my brother-in-law was lying there unconscious in a pool of blood. They had beat him up. So they called an ambulance and took him to the hospital.

While he was lying there unconscious in the hospital, the FBIs and sheriffs and [highway] patrols came, and it was like looking for a needle in a haystack. There were no tire tracks because it was a gravel road, and nobody could tell them what kind of car it was or what color it was. So there was no way to find them.

The next day my brother-in-law was still unconscious. So somebody said, "We'll bring a Chanunpa, and we'll pray for him so he could get well." That was good. So the next day my uncle and my cousins just happened to be there. So they all came together and performed this ceremony for my brother-in-law. So I showed them how it should be done. One man called the sheriff so he could sit in and listen also. So the sheriff came and sat in the ceremony with us.

That was a healing ceremony, but somebody prayed in there and asked who was responsible for beating up my brother-in-law. So the spirits answered that prayer. They told this person, "We could tell you, but we're not allowed to mention names. But we'll show you that we are spirits. We are going to backtrack those people, and we'll tell you about them."

Then we sang four songs in there. From here the spirits went over there and backtracked that car. Then they came back in.

When they came into the room you could hear this piece of tin falling on the floor.

They said, "You go south and from that point west. Then there's a big road leading from north to south. There's a big bridge and big creek there. Underneath that bridge we found that gun hidden there. From that point the car went and turned west again. There's a white house there. It's a little farm way out in the country. They parked that car in the garage and closed the door. So they hid it there. We went in and took the license plate. So we brought those numbers here. So from that you are going to find these five people."

So that's what we had heard hit the floor. Also they told us that there had been five people in that car. We turned on the lights to see, and there was a license plate lying there. So the sheriff took down the numbers. Then we turned the lights off again and sang the departing song. Those spirits took off. When we turned the lights back on, that license plate was gone also. But it was easier for that sheriff from there on.

After the ceremony, the sheriff went out and got into his car. He radioed in to have his detectives check the motor vehicle department for those numbers. They found out that this number was issued to an old man. After that they formed a posse and went to look under that bridge. They saw fresh dirt broken up there, so they started digging. They found that .22 rifle hidden there. They took that rifle, and that led to a lot of laboratory tests. They were looking for fingerprints and blood and what was the blood type and all that. They also saw that there was no firing pin on that rifle. So from there the sheriff went to that old man.

When the sheriff went there, they were gone. Nobody was home. The sheriff went into the garage, and here that car was in there. That license plate was back on there. It was the same number. From there it was easy. When they located that old man, he started telling them everything. That old guy had lent his car to his grandson that day. He told them what hours that kid took it. So that kid had taken the car and picked up his friends—four of them. They were running around and harassing people, because they were drinking and pot-smoking. So that's what they did.

The sheriff found blood stains in the car. The blood type there matched the blood found on the rifle. So there was a lot of detective work done on blood and hairs and tire tracks and like that. Then my sister recognized two out of those five boys in a line-up. She saw them, so she remembered them.

So it was sad. Looking at these young, nice-looking boys, you'd never think that drugs and alcohol would lead them to do such unimaginable things. After they were arrested, those kids, later, they cried like babies. Their fathers and mothers also cried because what their kids had done was not a pretty sight. These were good people, but their children were rotten kids. So it was really sad to see.

Anyway, we were able to doctor my brother-in-law in the hospital. Normally, when someone gets beat up [in the head] like that there is an aftereffect like paralysis. So the doctor thought that he would have brain damage. But it didn't happen that way. The next daybreak after we performed the ceremony for him, he just woke up like he had been sleeping. So the spirits fixed his brain again. He only had scars to heal. The scars are there, but he's back to normal again.

So it happens that way. When people get converted, they get shy and get away from these powers. Then, all of a sudden, something like this happens to them. All they have then are their prayers. But with this Chanunpa it is different. You can perform a ceremony, and the spirits will come in and diagnose—tell you what led to your problems or sickness. Then you can use that [information] to be alert so it won't happen again. But people aren't alert that way, so we lose them again. In an educated way they think this Chanunpa is a cure-all instrument. So they think it's okay to go back and start drinking again, because no matter what happens they think they can always come over here for some more hogie-pogie. So they have a false sense of security that way, because they don't really understand these powers. One time someone said to me in an educated way, "Well, experience is the best teacher." So I asked, "Well, who is that 'teacher' anyway? Is it Budweiser?"

So we learn a lot from the spirits that way. But if you come around with that shadow of a doubt in your mind, they are going to give you a lesson. So it's best not to come there to test the spirits, because they will test you instead. So, for example, we had this reporter come to the lodge. He was a journalist that had graduated from John Harvard University. He had come there because he wants to write about Indians. He was to write about the "sweat-lodge" and the "Sacred Pipe" and the altar and everything. Somebody sent him here, so he called and asked if he could come over. He was going to write a book about all this.

We were up in the mountains, so he came over there and sat down by the fireplace. He asked, "What's this fire?"

So I said that we call it *"seven fireplaces."*

"Well, how come? I don't see seven fireplaces, I only see one. So why do you call it seven?" He was talking that way.

"What kind of wood is that?"

So I told him it was pine.

"Well, what kinds of wood do you use?"

We use ashwood, cottonwood, hickory, and oak. Those are the four basic woods that we use. But we use whatever we can get ahold of also. We use anything that grows. Then I explained to him that when we burn those basic woods that smoke goes up and kills all the viruses. It purifies the air. But in the city there is a law that says no burning wood on air pollution days. When the pollution rate goes up you're not supposed to burn wood, so they want to get rid of all those wood-burning stoves. But when my people burn those four woods, it kills the viruses and purifies the air, yet the scientists call it pollution.

So, anyway, we talked about the fire, and he started writing cottonwood, ashwood, hickory, oak, and pine, like that. Then he asks, "Can you show me which one is the cottonwood?"

So I have to educate this Harvard University graduate, because they don't teach him anything about the green. To him a tree is a tree. So I point to a cottonwood down below and say, "That one way over there. That big one."

"Which one?"

"Well, that one down below."

So he wants us to walk over there, because he wants to see what it looks like. So I have to march him over there and bring him under that big tree. "This is called cottonwood."

"Oh, yes." So he starts writing. Then, "So can you tell me which one is the hickory?"

So I have to march him down there, and this one is the hickory.

Then, "Let's see. Which one is the ashwood?"

Well, that's about seven or eight miles down the road, and I'm too tired to walk that far. So I have to send one of my boys down there to cut one and bring it back for him. So it's really hard to train a Harvard University graduate. Green is green, tree is tree, rock is rock, and he's educated that way. So I have to lead him around to show him which one is which. It's really hard.

Then we talk about the rock. "What kind of rock is that?"

Well, that's a lava rock, basalt.

"Where do you get it from?"

From the mountain.

"Why is it called basalt?"

Well, it's from a volcano. At one time it was hot boiling mud, then it cooled off. So it's like this. The whole world was a volcano at one time. It was this ball of fire, and it cooled off and became minerals.

"Is that true? How do I find out about that? Who told you that?" He was talking that way. Then, "Where do you find this basalt?"

Well, over the mountain.

So he wants to go into the city to the county offices and get a map, because he's educated, see? He thinks that way.

So we went over there and went in. When we go in, there is this clerk there, and she says, "What can I do for you?"

So we ask for a map that shows where the volcanoes are.

She says, "I don't know. You have to ask the boss. They must have the maps here, but I've never seen them. I work here, but I've never seen a volcano."

That was kind of funny because the whole mountain right there was a volcano. But this clerk drives down the road there and never sees a volcano, and that's the way she's educated. Anyway, the boss comes in, and he shows us that all the time this whole mountain right there was a volcano. So we went over there and got some rocks.

Sometimes it's a lot of work to get those rocks. The next time we went to get rocks we went about two hundred miles west to Glenwood Springs [Colorado] and from there east to Basalt. That was the name of the town, Basalt. So we went on through there and stopped at a filling station. A young college boy was working there. I asked him where we could get some basalts. Well, he didn't know what basalt was. When we explained what they were, he said he didn't know where to find them but that there were some trailers down the road and we could go there and ask. So we went out the door, and by this time it was snowing. We went there, and there were three trailers sitting there. Some people came out and asked what we wanted, and we told them we were looking for volcano rocks. This guy said, "We don't know. I've lived here for eighteen years, and I've never seen a volcano around here."

So then we have to drag all the way back to Glenwood Springs, and then we have to drag south. So it got dark, and we were tired and cold, so we stopped and drank some coffee.

A policeman came and asked, "What are you guys doing?"

We told him we were hunting rocks. So he told us that he had a friend that was part Indian that got off duty in three or four hours and that he should know something. So he's a policeman, and he finished work around midnight. So we waited, and he came over.

He asked, "What do you guys want?"

So we told him we were hunting rocks. Anyway, it took about an hour and a half to explain to him why we were out there hunting rocks.

Finally he told us, "You go back to Basalt, and you turn left, and about one hundred yards there's a driveway there. Go down that driveway, and the whole side of the mountain there is a volcano."

So we went all the way back over there and got out with our flashlight. I was holding the flashlight, and we were kicking around in the snow. It looked like a bunch of snowballs there. So I picked one up. Yeah, that's it. Throw it in the truck. So while we were there this highway patrol car pulls up.

The officer gets out and says, "What are you guys doing out here at three o'clock in the morning?"

"Well, we're picking up rocks."

So then it took another hour to explain to him why we were picking up rocks at three in the morning. Finally, he turned on his spotlight and began to kind of help us.

"Here's one over here. Use that spotlight. Yeah, that's it. Good."

Then our tire went flat. And it's Thanksgiving Day. We saw a light at a station, so we drove, and they were still working there. We told them we needed a used tire, but they're an old style. So we have to go out back and look through all these tires while holding matches and cigarette lighters. Finally, we found the tire, so they fixed it for us. Then the other spare tire has a leak, so they found the break in it and put a boot in it. So we started for home, but it's too heavy in back so we couldn't steer the truck. So we stopped and put another guy in front. It was kind of hard for all of us to clam in there like that, but the front came back down. Anyway, we got home around eleven in the morning. So it's really hard to get stones.

Anyway, I had to educate this journalist, and he wanted to see where we got rocks. Then we went back to the camp, and next I had to teach him about the fire. We built a fire from the wood. You have to rub that wood together, or take out a flint and strike it, because that fire is inside the wood and the rock. (So I have some scientists now that are filming this to try to understand the origin of that fire. They are looking real close to see where the fire is.) But I have to teach this news reporter where that fire is in the rocks and the wood.

Then we built a lodge up there, and it's time to go to the altar. There we offer a little green—cedar, sage, and sweetgrass. Then we talk about Mother Earth, and I tell him how this sweetgrass is Mother Earth's hair. It is a perfume. When my grandma's spirit comes she carries that smell, that perfume, and you can smell it. That's why we use the sweetgrass as a prayer at the altar. So he learned about the sweetgrass. Then somebody instructed this journalist how to offer the "Sacred Pipe" so he could learn about the sacred powers. You have to have a reason for conducting a stone-people-lodge. Somebody has to offer the Chanunpa to the spiritual leader and state the reason why the Chanunpa is being offered. If he accepts that Chanunpa, then they have the ceremony. So this guy brings the Chanunpa to me and says, "I want to offer you a Sacred Pipe and ask Tunkashila to give me a power so I could report." That was his prayer.

When we went into the lodge that spirit came in. Then the spirit instructed that man that it was his turn to pray in the lodge. So he prayed.

"Oh, Tunkashila, I'm a white man. I'll never change colors, because I'm a white man. I could never be an Indian. No. No way."

He talked like that to the spirit. Then that spirit answered him the way he prayed.

He said [to me], "You tell him that he's talking about colors, but tell him that my life is red. Tell him that. Every living thing is red. My blood, my life is red. All the winged, four-legged, creeping-crawlers, mammals, fish-people, and two-legged, their blood is red. So tell him that my life is red."

When I translated to him what the spirit had said, he said, "Well, I just wanted to come here and make a report, you know. I just wanted to record about this pipe and the 'sweat-lodge' and make a report about the Indians."

So then that spirit said to him, "I'm a reporter also. I'm a scientist. I'm a doctor. I'm a lawyer. I'm an investigator, too. I'm a spirit, so I'm going to forecast what is going to happen. I'm going to report something to you to see how well you're educated and how well you've been trained. John Harvard educated you to where whatever you see, you have to report what you see. If somebody shoots somebody, you have to make a report. What you see, you have to report. So you're a reporter. So I'm a reporter, too, and I'll give you a little sample of how we report to test how you are going to report to the eyes and ears of the people. I'm a spirit. I'm sacred."

So that journalist had come over there to make a report on our sacred mystery powers. Before he went into that lodge he made a prayer that he would learn reporting. He wanted to test those powers. Now that spirit was going to test him. Then the spirit said, "There's a Korean jet flight number 007 that's going back and forth from Korea to Alaska. Tomorrow, at this time, they are going to punch keys on that computer, and later they are going to punch in the power. So that computer will be erased and cause that flight to go off course. And there is an imaginary line, it's called international line [national border], that is designed out of hatred and jealousy. That mark is not ours. That international law is not ours. So that flight will go off course and will go on the other side of that imaginary line and a lot of people will come down from the sky. So that's my report."

Now if this guy was educated, he would pick up the phone and say, "Hey, Korean 007, punch the power in first, then punch the keys. Then that flight will be on course." If he was smart, he would have believed that report. This was a spirit, and he told this guy that he was a reporter. So he was testing to see how well this journalist was going to make that report.

But this guy said, "Ah, I don't see how that could be. They've been going back and forth all this time. I don't see how a computer could make a mistake. Computers don't make mistakes. If I pick up the phone and make a report like that, then suppose nothing happens tomorrow. Then they're going to call me a liar. Damn liar. You know, they'll suspend me or take my license away. This is my bread and butter, so I can't tell a lie."

So he called the spirit a liar. But that spirit was testing him to see how well he was going to report to the ears and eyes of the people. But he opposed that report and rejected it.

"I don't see how that could happen. I don't see how a computer can make a mistake. Computers are always accurate."

So he talked that way. But me, I'm not the one giving that report to him. It's the spirit doing that. I'm just a dummy. I don't know anything, but I do understand what that spirit is saying, what he is trying to tell this guy. He offered a Chanunpa and wanted to have that power to report. He insisted that way. So if he was smart, he would have picked up that phone and made that spirit report to his people. He could have avoided that accident, and then he would have been an instant hero because the spirits gave him that power. Then he could have been elevated to a higher power because his prayer had been answered, and he would be contacting the spirit all the time. He could have been one of those big-time operators and hooked up to the satellite and televised all over the world. He would be announcing all the communications from the spirits.

This is what happened to him. But when we came out of the lodge, he rejected what the spirit had said. So the next day, in the morning, my boys went way down to town. It's a long way down from the mountain through dirt trails and washboard roads. In the winter time you need a four-wheeler to get up there. That evening the boys came back to the mountain. They brought a newspaper back, and the headlines read that Korean jetliner number 007 had been shot down from the sky because it crossed over that imaginary line. The Russians had followed that jet because it was off course, and two hours later they shot it down. So he could have saved those people.

At first, this journalist thought my boys had gone to one of those joke shops and had that headline printed on that paper. So he wanted to hear it on the radio. When he turned on that car radio, that report was on the radio also. So he took that paper and read it. Then he just dropped the paper and started pacing the ground back and forth. "I don't understand. I don't see how that could happen. I don't get it." He had called it a lie, but then that lie became real. So it became a truth.

So I was to educate this reporter, but now it's too much for him. So he tore up his notes and threw them in the fire and just sat there. Then he left. I don't know where he went. I've never heard from him. So there are a lot of people who write books about the American Indians. If you read a chapter, you get an idea about them. Then an hour later, if you read again, you're going to get another idea. So you close it, then read it again, and you're going to have another idea. So the secret and sacred of the Indians has never been revealed.

So those little things happen. That is why when the spirit comes I'm scared. I'm really scared! So I have to be like that dog—pull the ears down, put the tail between the legs, and really humble myself.

"Hey, Tunkashila, from these powers I have to speak from my heart. Come pity us and have mercy upon us. You know we're pitiful people. Give us health and help, because we don't know anything. We made some mistakes, so please forgive us. Let us do something good to replace the mistakes we made."

I have to pray that way. So I'm scared when that spirit comes. Don't think I'm standing there with my hands on my hips or banging on my chest saying, "Come here! I want to talk to you. What's this? What's that?" I'm not inquisitive. I just humble myself. I only pray for good things, because that spirit is the master. He could do anything, and you'll never know what he'll do. You can't make him do something you want him to do. You can't hate this guy and make the spirit hate him for you. You can't do that. You can't influence the spirit that way. You have to humble yourself and leave no room for that shadow of a doubt.

CHAPTER 8

The Eagle

One time I found this eagle lying on its back. We were driving down the highway, and I saw something lying on the side of the road. So we turned around and went back to see what it was. There was this eagle lying there that had been shot through. He was lying there alive. It had fallen and broken its wing. He tried to fly with it, but he was too weak. So I chewed a piece of sage and plugged his wound with it. I put some sprigs of sage around him, some on top and some underneath. Next I folded his broken wing and put a splint on it. Then I grabbed both feet, picked him up holding him to the west, and prayed. About halfway through he died there in my hands.

So we took him back to the stone-people-lodge. My dad and cousin were there with me. When we prayed, there was a flash of lightning, and the spirit of that eagle came into the lodge. He fanned me and touched me with a human hand. He thanked me for what I had done. There was a lump in my throat, and tears came to my eyes. He said, "When I was lying there bleeding in pain and slowly dying, you cradled me in your arms. You even patched my wound and prayed for me to live. But you also know that I have a spirit. I had no more blood, so I left. So now you have my robe here. Now I'm a spirit. So I came back to tell you that for doing that, for patching my wound and praying for me, for your love, I award you this feather. You are going to wear my plume. I promise that I will be hovering over you. I'll be in front of you. I'll be on both sides of you. I'll be underneath you." So that eagle spirit promised me that.

I didn't know how that [death] had happened to that eagle, so I asked Tunkashila what had happened. Then I heard the explosion of a high-powered rifle. It sounded like one of those stone-people [hot rocks] had exploded right there in the stone-people-lodge pit. I could hear that thump hitting the eagle's body. The bullet went through and then hit one of those sapling ribs of the lodge and ricocheted around—ping, ping—like that. Then the eagle said, "Now a *wasichu* put me on target for no reason at all. But I'm a spirit. I'm sacred. In four days you shall see." If I was educated, I would have asked, "Who? Who? Where? What?" and like that. Well, I'm not educated, so I understood what he meant. Then he told me that he now holds that power, that bang, that explosion, the power of that bullet, how fast that bullet travels. He said he was going to strike with that power.

So I prayed to him that I didn't want my people to get hurt. I prayed to him that way. So when I say "my people," I'm not talking only about my Sioux tribe from the Rosebud Reservation. I don't speak that way. I'm not an Indian from the United States. I don't think that way. I was speaking about the whole universe. I was speaking about all the two-leggeds, the four sacred colors that Tunkashila created. So when I say "my people" I'm talking about the black, the red, the yellow, and the white. That's what I mean.

When I told him that, he said, "That is so. Whatever you say is true. That is true. So I'm going to help. I promise I'll be above you, and I'll continue to watch over this land. And that threat of nuclear destruction, I will hold it there until there will be a time that your people will come together and decide not to toy around with this planet." So he promised me that.

So I wanted to repay my sympathies to Tunkashila. So I took the claws of that eagle and promised to keep them for one year. After one year from that day, I promised to pierce with those claws in the Sun Dance. The spirit came and said that that was good. He came over to me and with a human hand used the heel of it to wipe my tears. Then he rubbed my heart and back with both palms. He told me to take up courage and do what I had promised to do.

Four days later I was going along the same road where I had found that eagle. I saw a pickup alongside the road, and two elders were standing there. I stopped and got out. This man was lying there dead alongside a rifle. Those old people saw this man stop his pickup. There was an eagle sitting there on this haystack, and he got out of the pickup to shoot that eagle. His rifle was lying in the front seat. He pulled back and forth on his rifle by the barrel, and it went off. It shot him through in the same place the eagle I found had been shot through. So I knew it was the same man. So four days later I saw this, and it was sacred.

So we know these things. But there was a time that we couldn't talk about these powers. That was back in the 1920s and 1930s. At that time you would get in trouble for saying those things. But after I came back from World War II, I decided to talk about these powers. So one day I got up, and I was tired of this. So I said to myself, "I'm going to get up, and I'm going to tell the world that this Chanunpa is sacred." Just like that. So one day I got up, and I had a Chanunpa in my hand. "This Chanunpa is sacred of sacreds in this universe." So the first people that attacked me were these priests and all their members. So these were my people. They were my relatives.

So they said, "This guy is crazy. He talks about the devil. So he needs help." So they all signed a piece of paper that I needed to be examined by a psychologist. "We need a psychologist or psychiatrist to examine his head. If they find that he is crazy, then I think this guy needs help. So we are going to send him to a hospital to cure this guy. They know how to take care of him. So we'll just do that." So they went and told the judge. He told them, "So you sign a complaint." So they did that, and they made out a warrant for my arrest. So the sheriff delivered the warrant, and they arrested me.

So they brought a sack, and they put me in a sack. The sheriff said, "I'm sorry, but I have to take you in because there is a complaint. So I have to put you in a sack. They say you must be awfully crazy, insane. So they advised me to put you in a sack so you won't harm yourself or harm anyone, so you won't be a harm to the public. So I'm sorry, but it's just that I have a dirty job." So they put me in a sack. They call it a strait jacket.

So when they put me in that sack, they started kicking me around because I couldn't help myself. They threw me on the floor and kicked me and said, "You dirty Indian." Anyway, they started kicking me, and they cussed me; they pushed me. They sat me down in a chair, and somebody came and kicked that chair and kicked me over here. I couldn't help myself, so I hit my head on the floor. They were doing all this because the Christian people had complained about me. So it's a law. So they kicked me around because they hated Indians. So those police treated me really rough.

That Catholic priest and another minister were standing there by the door. I saw that one smile at the other priest. They were enjoying it. Anyway, they hauled me before the judge, and a doctor came there and started asking me some funny questions.

"So you think you're seeing something. Do you hear them at night? Do you see them in the daytime? What are they? Do you see snakes? Do you see animals?" He was talking like that.

Then he turned around and told the judge and the sheriff, "Well, this guy needs help. He doesn't even know he's sick, but he's sick in his mind. I think some of the things he went through might have caused this. Like he was in the war, and he helped to kill a lot of people. His record here shows that he was shell-shocked, so that might have done some damage to his brain. So that might have caused him to see things. Also, he's a medicine man, so he's been taking all kinds of drugs, and that's affected his mind."

Well, that's not the way it is. I don't eat those medicines. When that spirit comes in, he brings health and help. So when that spirit brings a medicine that you are supposed to administer, you have to isolate that person for four days and nights. That's really hard. Ninety-six hours is a mighty stretch. So when a person goes to vision quest you have to go four days and four nights without water or food. And that's where the medicine man is going to come to you. So that isn't a pill. You're not going to be sitting there eating dope or roots or those leaves they turn into the drugs that they are selling over here, like that cocaine. So they might think I'm sitting up there eating cocaine leaves or like that, but I'm not touching food or water when I'm out there. I'm not smoking marijuana or hashish or taking LSD. I'm not taking anything. But this doctor accused me that, because I'm a medicine man, I'm taking all sorts of drugs. So he said that all went to my head and made me haywire. That's what he told the judge.

So they talked it over, and then the judge said, "Well, you'll be sentenced to a mental hospital. When the doctors think you are clear, they'll release you. When your mind has been cleared, they'll release you to the public, or you might remain there for the rest of your life."

So they decided to send me to the funny farm. So then they said, "Okay, come on." Then they started shoving me again. I tumbled out of there and down the stairs. They opened the car door and threw me in the back. Nobody was there. Nobody said goodbye. Nobody prayed for me. Nothing. Those priests were there, and they started laughing. They didn't sprinkle those holy waters on me or burn that incense or say, "Jesus, cast this demon out and bless this man." Nothing like that, they were just laughing. So I was treated by Christian people that way.

So I was in the funny farm. Now a funny thing happened there. They threw me down in the basement. There was a room there. They took me out of that sack and shoved me in there. Then they slammed that steel-mesh door closed and locked it. There was a second door there that had a little window in it. They slammed that shut and locked it also. It had a big latch on it with a big padlock. So I looked around and began to crawl around in there. There was a bench in there, so I pulled myself up onto it. I hurt everywhere. My shoulder and elbows hurt. My knees hurt. Everywhere I got kicked, it hurt. Everywhere it hurt. I was sad. I was hungry. I was cold. Inside there the mats, floor, and everywhere was rubber, like little rubber points. And the bed was bolted down, and there was a mattress. There were no blankets or anything; it was just all one piece. The lights were imbedded into the wall.

So when I was inside, somebody came and started talking to me. He started comforting me, "Don't worry. Pray. Don't cry. Pray." I had heard this many, many times before that. This same spirit always came and consoled me. "I'm here. I'm a spirit. I'm here to help you. So don't worry. All the things you have been talking about are true. So you are a courageous boy. You have to take this route to bring the people you so love. No matter how bad they are, they are still people. You still love them. No matter what they did to you—they take things from you; they hurt you; they kill your people; they kick you around—you still love them. You're a courageous boy. So I'm here to help you." So he was talking that way. It seemed like some of the things he mentioned I knew or had heard before someplace, but I couldn't recall where it had happened. So I couldn't remember where it had happened or who told me, but it seemed like I knew before. Like somebody told me before or somebody said it before. I sort of had that feeling.

Then he said, "Come, I'll show you that I'm a spirit. Come on." Then he kind of brushed me. Then he unlocked those doors and pushed them wide open. So we walked out into the hallway. There were some little steps there that went up to a door to the outside. So we went up there and stepped outside onto the surface. There was a patch of ice there, crust, and snow. It was daybreak, and there was a black cloud there in the sky, and you could see the morning star. So we walked out there onto the snow. I couldn't see him, but you could hear him walk on that snow—crunch, crunch—and you could see his footprints there in the snow beside my prints as we walked along. So when we got out there, there was a man coming down from the clouds. So he came there, and those two met and started talking. So I was standing there and looking around—breathing and enjoying what all was around me. It was really good to take a breath and see all what Tunkashila had created and what Grandmother had given me. So this other spirit came from the morning star, and they started to visit. I heard them talking.

While I was looking around, each turned around and started back. So he brushed me and started walking back to the building—crunch, crunch. When I went down the stairway into the hallway, there were two doctors coming from one way and a nurse from the other way. They yelled, "Hey, Chief! You're not supposed to go out! Who opened the door? Who let you out?"

So I walked across the hallway and went back into that cell. Then those doors shut, locked, and that spirit that let me out was gone. Those two doctors came there, and one started to jiggle that lock. So the other one asked, "Did you lock it?"

He answered, "No, I didn't."

Then that nurse came there, and she started to jiggle that padlock. She asked, "Did either of you snap this lock?"

"No, we didn't."

Then she said, "But it's locked." So they were jiggling it around to see if it would come unsnapped.

Then they started yelling at me, "Who let you out? Who was it? You've got to tell me. Speak up! Who was trying to bail you out? Was it a white guy or was it an Indian? Who was it? How many people? Was it a woman or was it a man?" They were hollering like that.

So I said, "This man."

So they started looking around, but nobody was there. "What man?"

"Well, this man."

So they went somewhere and came back. Then Dr. Strong, the head of the department, came there with them. They came in and said, "We're not going to hurt you. You need help. You're a sick man. You don't know you're a sick man. We're going to help you." And that nurse kept telling me, "Think hard. Think hard."

Anyway, they took my pulse; they put a flashlight in my eyes; they looked into my ears and this and that. Later they took me upstairs. Then they all came there—all these psychologists, psychiatrists, "red cross" nurses, and staff—for a meeting.

Then the head of the department, asked me, "Did you go out?"

So I said, "Yes."

So he said, "Who took you out?"

I said, "That man."

"What man?"

"That spirit."

"What spirit?"

"That two-legged spirit."

"Well, who had the key? Did you have the key?"

I said, "I don't know. He just opened the door, and we walked out."

"Did you go outside?"

"Yeah."

"Who was out there? Was there a car out there? How many people were out there?"

I said, "Two."

"Who were they?"

"Oh, they came from a star. This guy came from the morning star, and they were talking. Then I came back in. Then those two doctors and the head nurse saw me. I heard them say, 'Chief, you're not supposed to go outside,' so I went back in. Then they came there and jiggled that lock."

Then he asked, "Who snapped it?"

I said, "I don't know. You should ask them, because I'm insane."

So after that meeting they decided they should bring an expert burglar to check those locks. So they brought this guy there and locked him in that cell. He had a little box there with all his little probing tools in it. So he tried to hook around and snap it open from the inside. But he couldn't get his hands through that wire mesh. So he fooled around there for about ten minutes, then he gave up. So Dr. Strong got really mad. So he said, "Okay, we're going to go back down there, and we're going to reenact the whole event."

So they did that. "Okay, where were you standing? Okay." So they put a little tape there.

"Okay, you stand there. Now were you taking long steps or short steps or fast steps?"

They were going on like that. So he got all those people in place, and then he took out a stopwatch.

"Okay, when I say *start,* everybody start walking towards the door. Okay, start."

Those three people came to the door and started jiggling that padlock. So that took seventeen seconds. So now an expert burglar had to use those tools to snap it shut in seventeen seconds, but that would be impossible.

So now Dr. Strong got even more mad. He said, "Okay, who

is crazy? Is Chief crazy or are these three people crazy?"

So then they took me to another room. While I was there, they did a lot of research. That's where they were doing their science. They talked about hallucinations with drugs, the chemistry language, and all this medical science—all that had been written. They were probing around there on guinea pigs or dogs or monkeys or Indians or whatever they were using for experiments. They wanted to know how people behaved. So they had all your history there, what war you were in, and like that. So nothing was left out.

Anyway, they finally got all the information there together. They even went over to the reservation and checked into my background, all what I had done. They found my dad, mom, sisters, uncles, cousins, and some of those people testified that they had come to the lodge and got well. So there were some witnesses out there. So when they came back, they put all this information together.

At the same time, they had a lodge for me back on the reservation. That gourd came over from there to visit me. He came right into that cell. He said that in four days I would be behind that altar with four classes of people there to judge if I was insane or not. So they were going to bring those people to a Chanunpa ceremony, and that spirit said he would be there to help me. So that gourd was going all over and talking at the same time. I was lying on that mattress, so he went this way and down to my heel, then up to the small of my back. When he got there, the doctors and nurses came there on their rounds, so he stopped and didn't say a word. He just laid there real still like. Now, how did he see them when I was lying on top of him? So he laid still.

Then the doctor said, "How are you?"

I said, "Oh, I'm okay."

Then he marked on his chart and left. When they went out, he started crawling up again. Then he said, "The medicine man is out there. We'll see you there." When he left, I looked out the window. I was on the second floor, but there was an Indian standing out there. He came over to the window, and the next thing he was standing inside.

He came over and said, "I'm a medicine man. I'm going to stay with you. We'll go back to the altar. I'll take you back to the altar. And we are going to bring these four classes of people there, and they are going to see for themselves that this Chanunpa is sacred. I'm a spirit. I'm a medicine man, and we're going to show them that this power is true."

So they had to bring four sane people to observe me, because I was classified as insane. So that's what happened. They released me from the hospital. They gave me a ticket and put me on a bus to go home. They had me under surveillance to see if I would try to escape. If I tried to escape, that would mean that I was insane. But I went back. They had notified my mom and dad, so they were waiting for me when the bus arrived.

My sister came there crying, "Brother. Brother."

My mom was saying, "Oh, my son. My son. Good to see you back here. I know you'll make it. You're courageous. Whatever it takes, I know you'll make it. You took a lot of beating, but you have the courage, patience, endurance, alertness, and all that it takes. All this was given to you. Now you have the power to bring all these brains that we have feared for hundreds of years. Now you bring them to the altar. I'm really proud of you. We're really scared, but you made us feel really good."

Then my sister said, "Let's go back. You know, really important people have come here. They all came in big shiny cars wearing suits. They're wearing white shirts and neckties and carrying briefcases. There are really important people here. Even white people came to see you. There's even a priest here. He's an archbishop. He came to see you. There's a doctor also. I heard that they are very important. There's even a scientist here. They said you were going to take them into a Chanunpa ceremony."

So I said, "Oh, good. Let's go."

So we went there, and all those people were there. There was even a representative from the legislature there. So all four classes were there—the scientific, the psychological/medical, legal, and religious-speaking people. So my dad let me fill the Chanunpa and display the altar. So I was setting up the altar, and there was a buffalo skull there and a little bunch of dirt. That dirt we go out and get from a mole hill. Then we put that dirt on the altar in a little circle like a pancake and place the tobacco ties around it.

Then we draw a picture in that dirt. There was also an eagle tail feather and an eagle plume there. And we had some claws hanging there and some robes hanging there on sticks. Also there was a shell there and a deer tail. And we had a piece of wood and a piece of stone. It's called *Chanunpa,* or "Sacred Pipe." We offer a little green in there.

So this priest was there, and he was checking everything out. He had a slurky smile on his face, and then he said, "You know, it seems like you're educated, but what you are doing here is 150 years behind civilization. You're going to have to change your tune, Black Elk, because we're living in modern times. We're living in the civilized, Christianized world now. We're living in the nuclear age. We're in the space age." He was talking like that.

So I said, "I don't know about being in the space age. It seems to me like we were airborne in the beginning. This earth, this rock is just floating around in space, floating around all the time. So I don't know about this being the space age." So those scientists started laughing at that.

Then he said something real funny. He said, "So why are you accumulating all those dead animals?"

It was really funny the way he said it, because I had never thought of it that way before. So I had a buffalo skull there and a deer tail and claws hanging there, but I never realized that I was accumulating dead animals.

So I laughed and said, "The day Tunkashila created them they are very much alive, so they will be here directly." So he sat down.

So we began. We turned off the lights and started playing that noisemaker, that drum—Chanunpa, honoring song, Four Winds, calling song, medicine song. Then—boom—a bolt of lightning, and that spirit came in. There was lightning and thunder inside and outside, and that eagle just swooped right in, flew right in. You could hear it and feel that wind. And there was rain also on the inside. Water dropped right through the ceiling, and it was raining on top of us. And there was a stove there that was still hot, and you could hear those drops of water hit that hot plate and go shooosh, shooosh, like that. Somebody said, "There must be a hole in that ceiling." When he landed, you could see this man in the pitch dark. But this priest, he was the most scared one there. He yelled, "Stop it! That's enough! I said stop it!" He was screaming at the top of his lungs.

Next, that buffalo came in.

"Oh, thank you, Tunkashila." You bless yourself by touching him.

"Oh, good. You're alive now. Thank you. Let us touch you and get well."

So he went over to that Christian guy and started poking him with his horns. That priest could feel something poking him, so he grabbed it and started feeling around in the dark. He could feel those horns. Then he felt this shaggy head and a shaggy hump. So he started yelling that there was a shaggy hump in there. I heard him.

"What is this? A buffalo! Get this thing out of here!" He was yelling that way.

So it was dark, pitch dark, but he could touch those buffalo horns and feel that shaggy head. That was really something for him, but we're used to it that way. I was educated in these spiritual ways, so I started thanking that buffalo for being there. So now you talk about Father, Son, and Holy Ghost. Now that ghost came in. But in this other educated way you have to see it and touch it first before you believe it. That priest, he believed it, but it really scared him to believe it.

Then the deer came in. His horns were lightning. He whistled and started pawing the ground. So that priest started grabbing those horns again and started feeling around. So that deer had come to the altar also. Then the gourd-people came in. They came to comfort and welcome everybody. Then they said, "The reason we brought these people is because of you. You prayed so hard. We told you when you were little about these powers, so now you took up the courage to tell the world that this Chanunpa is sacred. You had to go underground because all these people have been rolling over you. Religion, science, technology, military powers, and politicians all rolled together like a rolling pin rolled over this Western Hemisphere. So we came here to help you."

After I performed that ceremony those scientists said that maybe in 150 years modern civilization would understand these sacred powers. So I advanced 300 years in that ceremony, and those four sane people decided that I wasn't insane. So it's really funny. We've had a ceremony with a Christian, a scientist, a psychologist, a doctor, and even law-making people like a representative and a senator. It's really funny when you have those people inside. Even when they touch it and believe it, it really scares them. They're scared to go into Congress and say, "Well, a buffalo came in and an eagle swept right through the house." If they say that, they'll be sent real fast to the funny farm. But that's the way the spirit educates you.

Anyway, I kept those eagle claws. There is a ritual [Sun Dance] that goes with that piercing. There is a lot of preparation for it that must go on for a whole year in advance. By the following year everything had been prepared. We had the ropes, sage, buffalo skulls, prayer ties, and everything else was ready. We cut the sacred cottonwood tree. It took fifteen people to carry it up to the site. Then the site was laid out. The spiritual foods—water, corn, berries, and meat—were all in order. Everything was facing west. The tree and altar were aligned from east to west, the way the sun moves. I lay down from north to south. Then my brother pierced me. I want to recommend to you that you never do this out of curiosity because it is connected with death and life. So when he pierced me with those eagle claws, it seemed like there was this force pressing against me. There was this cracking sound, and I felt like he had broken one of my ribs. Then it felt like this pin piercing my heart. I knew then what piercing the heart meant. My heart stopped, and I stopped breathing. I couldn't blink my eyes. I couldn't move. I lay there frozen, like I was petrified, but I was conscious.

Then I looked in the direction of the sun. It appeared really huge and bright. Then the sun became a black polka dot, and it dilated. Different colors began to appear—blue, green, orange, red, and like that. Each time a different color appeared until there was a complete rainbow that appeared around the sun, a circular rainbow. Then as I looked up into the blue sky, a hole appeared in the sky like a big window. Then a man appeared in the window. He had both arms stretched out full. And I could see feathers in between. There were also tail feathers that fanned out and came down. They were coming down real slowly, like sinking. He wore a red robe. It slid over his shoulders and tied around his waist. Then out of nowhere a cloud vapor formed, like dust and smoke. It started getting thicker, and I could see lightning and hear thunder. Then a bolt of lightning that was rapidly moving up and down began to slowly descend to the ground. Then that man started walking down the bolt of lightning and landed right beside me.

Then he said to me, "Tunkashila heard you, so he sent me here to deliver a message. Tunkashila sends the news that this long island [North and South America] still belongs to you Earth People. This Chanunpa that you are holding is very, very sacred. This land is still sacred. So tell it to each other, that you shall live forever." So I got that blessing for honoring the spirit of that eagle that was shot to death.

The first time I experienced thunder, lightning, and those clouds all around was on a vision quest. Those clouds bellowed up to about sixty thousand feet in height. Then a black cloud rolled in underneath, like a black robe. It spiraled around and formed a doughnut. There were different colored lights all around—green, pink, orange, and yellow lights. The wind made a tremendous sound, and you could feel this suction like a giant vacuum. Hot air would come, then cold air would come, and sometimes it was still. When it was hot, I would be standing there sweating and wringing wet. Pretty soon it would shift. First, kind of a lukewarm air, then it would get ice cold. Then it would shift back.

At the same time there was this sound like gravel sliding down a tin chute. The sound was like that. I was praying, and then all of a sudden I looked up. I saw lightning, and it began to spiral down. As it started coming down, all the clouds wrapped around it. It was a spirit coming down. I heard a voice say, "Now [the power of] Tunkashila. They are going to show you a power. So be steadfast. Pray." So I was standing there praying as that black robe wrapped around and spiraled down. When that black robe came down, it brought the black light, and it was pitch dark. Pitch dark. There was a light on top, like a floodlight. Then a man appeared. He jumped right in. He was a figure like us, only he was all black like a shadow. And his eyes were purple. They were blazing—blue, green, orange, and like that. So I was scared.

Then he said, "Tunkashila hears you, so the Thunder-Beings elected me. They appointed me to come here and see you and show you a power."

So I said, "Ho. Thank you."

Then he came over and said, "That Chanunpa you hold is very sacred. I am a spirit. I am sacred. I was appointed and elected to come to see you and show you a power."

I answered again, "Hi-ho."

Then he came over and touched my eyes. Then he touched my nose, touched my arms, touched my fingers, and touched my toes. When he let go of me, I could see everything as though it was broad daylight. And that scares me! So that was the power that he showed me.

Then he said, "You pray to the bright light. You pray to this black light. I'm a spirit. I'm sacred." Then he went back up into the clouds and disappeared. As soon as he left the altar, that black light came back. So I learned these things that way. So I realized that there was a black light as well as a bright light.

So now I have that eagle power. It took a long time to get that power. I prayed for seven years. Each year I went on a vision quest for four days to pray for the people. So on the last vision quest, the first three days and nights there was nothing. Everything was quiet. Normally at our place there are lots of owls and coyotes. They sing songs, bark, and howl every day. We see them every day. You could see those owls sitting on a tree, but even they were quiet. Even the wind was quiet. I didn't hear or see anything. When the fourth day came, boy, now I was going down. I was standing out there in the sun. Boy, it was hot. Later, they told me that it was 115 degrees that day. So that's really tough. You stand out there in the sun for just three or four hours, and you'll find out how tough it is. I had been there for four days. So I began to pray. While I was praying, I heard a whistle. I heard it way up there someplace. I looked up, but I couldn't see anything. So I kept praying. Then I heard it again. I scanned the blue sky but saw nothing. About the third or fourth time I heard it, I could see it coming. It was an eagle. Now my heart started pounding. I knew he was coming to me. I could see him coming closer and closer. He was coming down in circles. When he tilted this way, he disappeared. Then as he banked around, I could see him again clearly. So I prayed and prayed.

He landed in front of me about twenty-five or thirty yards away. Then he started walking towards me kind of wobbly like. His wings were half folded. Then all of a sudden I saw him lift his face. He rose up, and he was like us. He walked fast and came up to me. The first thing he said was, "Tunkashila hears you, so he sent me here. I'm a spirit. I'm sacred. That Chanunpa you're holding is very *wakan.*" Then he said, "I was here. The powers of the Four Winds wear those robes. They are standing all around you. They are converging around you. These past days they have been watching you. They have been listening to you. That's how come they were quiet. They honor you."

To prove that, he revealed everything I had said on the first day. He even answered my prayers. Then he revealed every word I had said on the second day, then the third day, then the last day. So he repeated and answered every word I had said there up to then. Then at the end he said, "Now you are going to begin to pray." Well, I thought I had been praying like heck for the past four days. Now he said I was going to begin to pray. I never questioned it—Why? Why? Why?—like that, but I caught it. I heard it loud and clear. So I prayed silently. Then he said, "They're coming after you now. That is so." So he started running. Boy, he was really going. Just then my dad and grandpa came to get me, so they saw that eagle taking off. He went back up and disappeared. They said, "Oh, good. You did well."

So they took me back down to the lodge. Everyone was milling around there waiting for me to be brought back down. They all wanted to hear the spiritual news. They were eager to hear the firsthand information. So we went into the lodge. When I prayed inside that eagle spirit came in. If you have any questions, that's the time he will explain things to you. So then it was explained to me what he had meant. When he had said, "start to pray," I thought he meant I hadn't been praying. But that was the educated way of thinking. So what he meant by "start," we have a word for that, was to carry out that prayer. What he meant was that I was to walk pray. Pray walk. Walk with my prayers. So everything I prayed for, I would have to walk with those prayers, not lay them down and walk on them. What I prayed for, I had to live with. Everything I prayed for would fall in line—in place one at a time. So I explained how I understood it then.

Then the spirit said, "That's good. You understand. Good. Thank you."

The last word he said was, "From East to West those *wasichus* are flooding this land with bad water [alcohol]. The four ways of life, the four colors, are all becoming friends to that bad water. The first thing that does is distorts and twists people's minds. It hurts people's feelings. Then it destroys their brain cells and does damage to the organs and structure. It weakens the spirit. So it makes bad relations. People hurt each other by shooting and stabbing. Some commit suicide. Then some homes, nests, are broken. People get divorced. People die on the road. They create orphans. Others end up behind prison bars. Hatred and jealousy are threaded into those steel bars, those steel doors. But there will be a time I will come and pull the thread out, and there will be no more prison doors. So for that, I denounce the taste of that bad water. I don't even like the smell of that bad water. So you are going to be my friend."

So I said, "How. Thank you." I agreed because I understood. It was all packaged and explained. Everything was scientific and logical. Everything was self-explanatory. So I agreed. Then he thanked me and left.

So it took me seven years, seven vision quests to obtain that power. I gave that back to my people, because I had prayed for the people. So it's kind of hard to pray for people with the Chanunpa. I want to help people. I want to do something good for them. I want to learn something good, too. At least one time in my life, I want to do something good for people. So I have one little credit to my name, or in his name, in his power. So when he comes, I've done something good, or I saved somebody's life that way. So I have the prayers and answers with it. So all the blessings were given back to me many times over. They even filled over. So these powers that were given to me, they can't be evaluated in terms of money. They cannot be measured. So I say thank you. I thank my grandpa, dad, mom, my relatives that way.

That way my people will live to see another day or another moon or another year or another generation. I want to keep that nuclear destruction standing by, so we'll live another generation. So my prayers were answered. Otherwise, some idiot could push a button and annihilate everything. Then we wouldn't have a home. So now it's on standby. We're standing by because our lives are at stake.

So in my request, praying for the people, Tunkashila was good enough to send a delegate, a representative of his power to communicate that what I said was true. What our prayers demanded was right. It is true. That's the way Tunkashila wants us to be. So he never gained anything back from us. We create that bad among ourselves. We create it; then we try to call it devil, Satan, or evil. But man creates it. There is no devil. Man creates the devil.

So when you go to vision quest, you go there because Tunkashila is the Creator, and [for] Grandmother. She gave birth and life to all the living. So Grandfather and Grandmother are one. When you understand that, when it is fully organized in your mind, then you make your commitment. Those spirits will come and reassure you. But I don't command anybody. I can't say, "Hey, you go there for four days." I can't say that. I don't do anything. I don't bless feathers. I don't bless the Chanunpa. I don't bless anything. But I pray for people that are going to carry that feather, because I know that that eagle is sacred. He is *wakan*. But I can't make him *wakan*. I don't have that power. I'm just barely making ends meet, so I can't make an eagle more sacred. But I do pray for people, and I instruct them, because with the little experience I have, just like the blink of an eye, I understand that power of the eagles. That's why they gave me that sacred name, Little Eagle. So Little Eagle is my spiritual name.

CHAPTER 9

Everything Was Dying around Me

Most people don't understand *hanbleceya*. If I were to explain it real deep, that would take maybe two or three days. To really understand it, you have to go up there on the hill and be isolated. Like I have gone on many vision quests. Each time the spirits tell me when to go. They also tell me where to go. So there were times that I was scared, too, but I had to go. I had to carry out this vision.

It may look like it's real simple, but it's not simple. It's really tough. At those times I have to have courage, I have to have patience, I have to have endurance, and I have to have alertness. All these four you have to have to be an Earth Man. So I learn, too. When I go on vision quest, I stand before Tunkashila. I wear a robe, and there is no eating of food. I go there and hold the Chanunpa in my hands. Then the wisdom, knowledge, power, and gift are in my hands. In other words, the "In God We Trust" is in my hands. So I respect and I love.

When you go inside that power, there's no fear. It's so beautiful! There's no fear there. There's no pain. You won't even feel that fire. That fire will comfort you—cool, lukewarm, warm, like that. And the scent is so beautiful. You could smell it. It's really beautiful! So when I go there, I could say anything.

There was one vision quest I went on, and everything was dying around me—everything—animals, old people. Everything. So some of these fish came to the shore, and they died. So I prayed for them. And my people were dying all around me. So I started to pray.

"Grandpa, Grandma, there are sadnesses and worries and sickness and pain and death. There are as many as there are grasses growing around here," I said.

While standing there, I was dying also. I was draining down—going down and down. I knew I was dying. I was standing up there for four days and four nights, and now I couldn't even stand up. I knew I could no longer go on like this forever. I knew everything was dying around me. I was dying. Not only just me, but all my people were dying. Not only Indians, but I know the Red Nation will die. I know the Black Nation will die. I know the Yellow Nation will also die. I know all the White Nation will also die. So that power is coming. The silent death is approaching us from behind. When the spirit came, he told me that. He said, "That silent death is approaching you from behind."

So I understood all this, what he was saying. I was educated in that way. So I began to pray, so that the power could relay the message. I was just lying there and praying.

"Tunkashila, you're the Creator. You created everything that is around me. You created the white and black and red and yellow people. We're all standing on one universe. But there's problem after problem—sadness, sickness, and pain. All the trees and all the green are dying. Animals, winged-people, everything is dying around me. And I am dying. My people are dying. We cradle them in our arms and rock them. We ask, plead for their life, but they die in our hands. We have to bury them. So the whole world is a cemetery.

"So I'm sad. You gave us this land to live on. This is where the peace lives. Now these people [Western civilization] came from all directions here, and now they took everything away from me. All that is left of me is my robe and my spirit. Now I'm dying. I gave everything away. I don't have anything to give you anymore. Only my robe and my spirit are in your hands. Now my tears come."

I was thirsty, so I put sage in my mouth. There was no water, but at least I had sage in my mouth. Then there was a wind. The air was cool and kind of lukewarm. Just about the time I would get too warm, there would be a nice little lukewarm wind coming. Then there was cool air, ice cold, and before I would get chilled another little lukewarm air would come and warm me. It was going that way. It was like breathing on me. Then there was a perfume. That wind had a beautiful scent. It smelled like sage, cedar, sweetgrass, sunflowers, and fruits. All those scents were there. You could even smell the fruits. Oh, it was just beautiful!

Then all of a sudden I heard somebody. Then Grandmother, she came. There was a light. She carried a cane [staff], and there was a crystal, a stone, on the top of it. There was light all around that stone. She came, and she was so beautiful! I was weak, tired, hungry, cold, sick, dying. I couldn't even get up. I couldn't help myself. I was just lying there, and all of a sudden I saw a light. It was a light like maybe as big as a room. Like a beautiful light. So I got up. When she came, she planted that cane in the ground, and that light went all the way around me. It was all colors, rainbow colors. It was really beautiful!

Then everything came to life. I forgot I was tired. I forgot I was worrying. The ache and the pain went away. That all went away. I didn't even remember it going away. I was so happy and so alive. I was so glad to see my Grandmother this time.

I said, "Grandmother."

She answered, "Yeah."

Then "Grandmother!"

"Yeah!"

"Grandmother?"

"Yeah?"

She followed that tune. Whatever way I said it, whatever expression I used, she used the same [intonations]. She was following me with that tune like that.

I couldn't express myself. I couldn't express that feeling that I had. I couldn't say anything more—just "Grandmother" over and over. I was so happy to see her that I couldn't add any more.

So finally she said, "Grandchild, that Chanunpa you are holding is very sacred. Tunkashila, the Great Spirit, is watching you.

And the powers of the Four Winds, they're wearing these robes, and they're watching and listening to you. So grandchild, pray."

Then I remembered why I came there. Oh, yeah, I came here to stand before Tunkashila. So I said that universal prayer, "Grandfather, Grandmother, to the four cardinals of the universe, between the earth and sky—to the Eagle Nation and down to the stone-people—and the circle to all my people. Thank you. Thank you. I bring sacred food here. I bring offerings here. Let my people rest. Take care of them. Cradle them in your arms. Wipe my people's tears and cradle them. Take their spirits in your arms and wipe their tears. Forgive their iniquities and set them free. So now in spirit my Grandpa and Grandma come. My people are now in good hands. So I thank you very much."

So it's really hard to say thank you when my Grandpa and Grandma died. My tears came from a long way down in my throat, and I couldn't swallow. There was a pain in my chest. I had gone without food and water for a long time. Then when the spirit came, when my Grandma came, I really felt good. So I started to laugh and cry at the same time. This never happened to me before, but it did happen to me then. I laughed at the top of my lungs—screamed, yelled. At the same time, I cried. So it never happened to me before, but it happened then.

So I remembered why I went there—for health and help. You offer those sacred foods to the Four Directions, then up and down. So the spiritual food offering is sacred. Those bowls of food there are sacred. So everything you bring to the altar is an offering, like that water, corn, berries, and meat. When you bring it there, that spiritual power is put in a reserve, and it will grow. Those trees, they hold water. The grass and all the herb plants, and all the flowers—all this—will grow again and will multiply again. And more fruits will blossom and flower. The flower fruits will grow sevenfold. And all this will continue to breathe, so that we could breathe oxygen again. The spring water will come, so we will have water to drink. The green will produce food and fruit for our little children to eat.

So I forgot all my pain. I forgot that I had been up there for four days and four nights, and that I was craving for a pizza or 7-Up, like that. Now that's all gone. I'm energized because of that spirit power. My flesh digests those flavors, the scent. My skin absorbs and digests. My eyes digest what I saw. My sense of smell digests through my whole system. Like when you see food, you crave for it, and your mouth starts to water. It was like that. So when I started praying with that green, that sage, in my mouth, there was a little water spring that broke underneath my tongue. The water just sprung out, and my mouth started watering. And I began to sense, smell. It was sweet, and it was sour. Oh, it was really beautiful! I could taste, and I could smell those fruits out there. So inside that water there was a scent and a flavor. I could taste that flavor. Then there was more water. When I started moving that sage around in my mouth, maybe I was craving for apples and pears, because I could taste them in my mouth. Then I started chewing on the sage, and it felt and tasted like I had a piece of meat and fat in my mouth. Then when I was drinking, swallowing, it was like I was drinking soup. So I was educated that way. It's unbelievable! If I tell this to scientists, they'll send a specialist to examine my head. So it's really funny the way I learn things.

Anyway, I started to pray. It was like drinking water and eating green. I could smell it. Like all the green was there. Like at one point it was like I was eating celery or something like that. I could chew it. I could feel it. And so I began to pray, "Oh, thank you, Tunkashila." So I learned this from a spirit. I got strength. So I was able to sing and pray for all my people that were dying around me.

When I finished, she said, "Thank you grandchild. Thank you. Thank you."

Then I took the sacred food offerings and prayed with them. I gave her that spiritual food there right from the wooden bowls.

Then she said, "Heyeee. Heyeee. Grandchild, I'm very hungry. Thank you. Thank you." That's what she said. Then she took it out of my hand. What she took was the scent, the flavor, the taste that is in there. That's what she took. It's not to fill her tummy. It's not that way. Then she blessed me for it. Then I offered it to Tunkashila and to the people. Then I took some.

Then she said, "I took this food and your prayers and what you said. I take this and tuck it under my arm. And I will go.

When I go back there, Tunkashila always returns it [your offerings/prayers] to you four times, but now this time Tunkashila will return everything to you seven times back. Everything that you stored in there and gave honor to will be returned to you seven times."

So I thanked her. It really made me feel good. Boy, it was, you know, really good!

Then she said, "And there will be a time that this water and the green will go back to earth. The effect will be that all the winged, four-legged, and the same with the two-legged, will starve to death."

So who's going to starve to death first? It's the people from the multinational corporations. It's those genius people with the highest intelligence. It's those who own the highest and own the biggest. It's those who accumulate the most gold and material wealth. They are the first ones that are going to starve to death. They are the first ones that are going to die. Even if they hoard and store all that food and protect it with machine guns, tanks, rockets, and poison gases, that won't help. When they open those cans, there will be nothing but maggots inside.

Then the heat will be so intense that they will be cooked alive. So there are no shelters. There are no atomic fallout shelters. And the ones that stored that water and food and all the pills inside and put all that on spring shockers like inside a bedspring, they are the first ones that will be cooked. So I got scared. I got really scared! Then Grandmother reached down and gathered up some dirt in her hand. She held it up and began to let the grains of sand fall from her hand.

She said, "Grandchild, I have love for you this many."

Now nobody could count that many grains of sand. So I knew then that Grandmother had endless love for us. I understood that.

Then she said, "Now, tomorrow at noon you hold up your Chanunpa, and, Tunkashila, they are going to show you a power." Then she left.

So the next day at noon I held up my Chanunpa. Then an orange light was coming towards me like a tube or a telescope. It was getting smaller and smaller. Then there was a little tiny spark that landed in front of me and hit the ground. It bounced up and hit me and then bounced back. When it hit the earth, there was another light. Here it was broad daylight, but there was another light. Then I could see right through those big rocks and big trees there. When I looked at my hands, I could see right through my hands. You could see the outline, and the bones and veins were like little shadows. It was like when you take an X ray. It was something like that. I could see through myself like I was cellophane.

Then when I looked down, I could see right through this world. I could see the stars on the other side. That really scared me. So there was another power there that made the atomic bomb look like one match stick. The people with those atomic bombs, we call them a superpower, but I call them super insane because that is going to lead us to mass murder and suicide. So we're buying it, and paying for it, all in the name of "In God We Trust." So now I'm getting scared. But Tunkashila is so merciful that he allowed me to take a glimpse of his power; otherwise I would have evaporated and disintegrated when that power came.

So I thanked Tunkashila. Then I prayed and begged for our life.

"You're the Creator, but man by some unknown power twisted his own mind and took that power. He took rocks and melted them. Then he formed and shaped things. We call this talent *technology*. Now we've gotten to the place where we're attacking your creation, and we're attacking our Mother with those tools. We make destructive tools. But those tools were made out of bad thoughts and bad words. So we misused your wisdom and knowledge and power. So now we are going to kill ourselves by toying around with your sacred powers. So, Tunkashila, you're the real amnesty. Amnesty means forgiveness. You are the only one that could forgive. But I cannot sacrifice one spirit. I cannot condemn or even give one spirit away, because you are the Creator. So you could forgive, and I cannot afford to lose one spirit. So, Tunkashila, you are so merciful that you could forgive our iniquities and wipe our tears and set us free. Tunkashila, I beg you. I plead to you this way."

Then I heard a Voice up there. There was thunder and the scratching sound of a bolt of lightning. Then a Voice came out.

It just boomed out. It was so huge and so strong that I was shocked at first. Then a feeling drifted over me, and I felt really good. I knew it was the first time I had ever heard the direct Voice of Tunkashila! And the Voice said, "Grandchild, I stand here watching you and listening to you. Everything that you tell me is so." So I heard from the Thunder, and I really felt good. Then the powers of the Four Winds brought those spirits from all directions. They were the spirits of our ancestors.

So we know from prophecy handed down nineteen generations ago what is going to happen to those spirits. They have to wait for the seven whistles. The powers of the Four Winds take them to the West where there is a spiritual camp. They will stay there until the seventh whistle sounds. So far, four whistles have sounded. We are in the fourth whistle now. Now those [last three] whistles will follow one right after another. Before the fifth whistle, the Earth will shake, and tall buildings will tumble down. Countless people will vanish. So if the West Coast of this Turtle Island caves in, what is going to happen to all those nuclear power plants? On the sixth whistle the fire will come, and all life will cease. Then the seventh whistle. When that whistle sounds, Tunkashila will appear, and Grandmother, she's going to awaken. The whole Earth will vibrate. Thunder and lightning will echo throughout the solar system. All the star-nation-people will come, and there will be countless people coming from the sky. So all the dead will resurrect, and they will be here. And Grandmother, she will appear in our midst. And Grandfather will appear. It will be the first time that we are going to see the face of Tunkashila. Those who see his face will live forever. So that is the definition of the Earth People. That is why I am here. So Tunkashila answered my prayer and extended our time so that we could avoid that nuclear destruction.

Then Grandmother came, and she said, "Ho, grandchild. They are coming to pick you up now. So finish your thank-you prayer. Say thank you and go back. And stay behind this Chanunpa. And tell those people to love each other, and stay behind this Chanunpa. Use me as a shield. That stone [bowl] is me. There will be no bad words or thoughts that can come into you, because that stone will shield you. Bad words will hit and ricochet off. They won't penetrate. They won't get to you. Hatred and jealousy run parallel to this Chanunpa, so stay behind it and you'll never be touched by hatred and jealousy. Tunkashila promised to put an electrical fence, an electrical power, around you. The silent death is approaching from behind you, not from the front. So when you return, tell those four ways of life—tell those white people, tell those black people, tell your people, and tell those yellow people to love each other and stay behind this Chanunpa. So go back and tell them." That's what she said.

So I said, "Oh, thank you." Boy, I was really glad that I had finished.

Then she said, *"Hecetu,* that is so." Then she disappeared.

Then my dad, sisters, and relatives, they all came. They came up and took me back from that mountain. They took me back to the lodge. They even brought a canvas up there to put me in, in case I was dead or had to be dragged back. So they were prepared to drag me back down. But here I was alive and still kicking. So they wondered how come I wasn't tired. Here I was very much alive, so they were really appreciative.

After I came back, some of that sacred food was left. So some sick people came there and took a little piece. That little pinch digests in your mind, your hearing, seeing, smelling, tasting, and feeling. It goes all over. And that scent is still there. It goes around this whole world. So you take a little taste—aaahhh—that flavor you smell. Then you're no longer tired. That pain also goes away. So that is the way Grandmother prayed to me. So I brought back one little piece of the knowledge. It was beautiful.

So I've experienced what the vision quest is all about. Like we have that radio technology going right through here. You have a little gadget, and you turn it on, and it will come on, see? But if you sit here and try to hear the radio just with your ears, you don't hear anything. And there's a color TV going right through here. If you close your eyes and try to see it with your mind's eye, you'll just see a blank. But when I went to one vision quest, I was sitting in a hole. In fact, I was hanging in there. I was pierced two in the front and two in the back. So I was hanging inside. It was kind of painful. Blood was dripping down, and I was trying to figure out what caused this pain. I could feel that blood clear down to my toes. So they call me dumb, and maybe I am dumb. Maybe they're right. Or maybe not. Maybe it's the other way around, like that, you know. This was going through my head.

Anyway, the spirit came in. He said, "We're going to show you the power. We are stone-people. We are sacred. We are going to let you see."

Then my mind's eye opened. I could see the whole universe. I could see the surface. I could see the buildings. I could see the highways. Then he shifts over here, like opening the clouds, and I could see all these glittering lights. Then he said, "These are powers we gave to man, but now they've misused them."

Then they showed me another power. Now I could see all the color TVs. They were all overlapping. Like when a TV goes sideways, you see those long faces, or like that. You could see people banging or screaming. Some were pretend laughs, and some were pretend cries, and some were real hurt cries. So I was in there watching color TV. They let me see it. So when they opened my mind's eye, I could see that color TV going right through there. So I was watching. And I could see the radio waves coming right through there. They changed me so I could hear all the radios. It sounded like two or three stations jamming in there. I could hear it. Then I could hear the telephone cables humming. It was a continuous humming. And inside, I could hear them talking. So I could also hear the telephone conversations that were going on.

Then a funny thing happened to me in that hole. A telephone rang inside. I thought that was really funny, because the spirit had hooked me up with a telephone in there. It went ding-a-ling, ding-a-ling, like that. I stood there, and I thought that was funny. So I said, "This is Black Elk recording." Then I heard a conversation going on. At first I couldn't make it out. Pretty soon I kind of tuned my ears and tried to catch a word. All of a sudden, a man's voice came out real clear.

He said, "Is it true that those we call Indians, do they actually have powers?"

That's what the voice said. Then, next thing, a woman's voice came out and said, "That's what we learned. So we should look into it and investigate." That's what the woman's voice said. Then it was gone.

That made me think. It seemed like the men always had doubts as to whether my people really did have the power to communicate and listen to the spirits. But that woman said that was what she learned. So it seems that the women always have the power to look in and investigate. Anyway, I was watching those highways and roads. There I saw semi-trucks with false labels on top or on the sides. I could look inside, and there were nuclear warheads and plutonium and all this little stuff they were hauling around to make destructive tools. The people standing there didn't really know what was going on, but I could see what was being carried inside those false labels. So you can't fool Tunkashila. Maybe it said on the outside it was a milk truck, but those deadly chemicals were in there. They were hauling those trailer houses, but there were nuclear warheads in there. They had big white signs behind it and yellow lights.

I could see those trains. Inside they were hauling all those deadly chemicals, nerve gases, and nuclear wastes. They were going right through the middle of those towns. Millions of people were living there, and they were going right through. Suppose one of those trains derailed and dumped all that junk right in their front yard. It could happen that way, see? So the people, they didn't know what was going on. Those people living there were blinded by those false labels on there. But I could see inside. I could see what was really in there. So that scared me, because that's the way Tunkashila sees everything. So you can't fool the eyes of Tunkashila. You can't hide anything from Tunkashila. So that scared me. But this was done undercover, so the people didn't really know what was going [on] around there.

Then the spirit said, "Now we are going to show you another power." He moved his hand across his face, and, again, it was like a cloud opened. Then I saw countless spirits. They were just roaming around, just floating around. Some were standing along the highways where they had been killed in a car. They were just standing there. They didn't know which way to go. Most of them were where those junk cars are piled up. They were just milling around. Some of them went into churches and stood there. People were going by, but they didn't see them.

Then I saw those back alleys and dark ways. There were spirits there just roaming around. Then I saw a crossroad, and this car weaved off and hit another car. People were lying there full of blood. Then they stood in shadow and joined those spirits that were just roaming around. Some of those church people were saying, "May the Lord lead those on Earth to the gates of Heaven." But that spirit was still just roaming around there. Or somebody committed suicide. Then they would say, "Oh, that belongs to the devil. We don't need to say a prayer over it. Burn it up and spread the ashes." They'd say something like that. But those spirits, they didn't go to Heaven, and they didn't go to hell. They were just floating around.

Then I saw a spiritual camp [where West ends], and my people were there. I heard a drum. I heard a whistle, and I saw the smoke. I could hear kids screaming and laughing at the top of their lungs.

Then the spirit said, "We're going to show you another power." Then they showed me the power of the drum. When you pray with that drum, when the spirits hear that drum, it echoes. They hear this drum, and they hear your voice loud and clear. It's like amplified. Like you get on the microphone, and it amplifies throughout the whole canyon. So the spirit could hear you. They could recognize your voice also. I recognize lots of voices. So that's the way it is with the spirit. They recognize your voice. So when you're praying with that drum, your voice is amplified [via the drumming], and the spirit can hear you. Then they closed that part.

Then the spirit said, "Now, we're going to show you another power." When he moved his hand, it was like a dimmer. Like you go into a house, and you turn that little knob, and it dims. When that dimmer was turned on, there was a fire that came, and everything just evaporated. So when that light turns on there will be a tremendous degree—countless millions of degrees Fahrenheit. Everything that light touches will just evaporate. So that really scared me. So I was there holding the Chanunpa, and I prayed for my people. I sent a voice to Tunkashila.

I said, "Tunkashila, I don't want to lose even one spirit,

because you are the Creator. You created the White Nation, the Black Nation, the Red Nation, the Yellow Nation. You created all of us. So I can't afford to lose even one spirit." I prayed like that. So I learned all this hanging there [in that hole].

One time I went to the south [Texas] to vision quest. It was right there in the desert where all those cactus are growing there. Boy, that was a tough one. Everything was wild there. When we were driving there in the pickup, even those Brahmas came and charged us with their horns down. Then they dropped me off. They placed me there, and then they left. I had a Chanunpa. You can't run from there, because there are thousands of different shaped cactus there. So I stood there.

There was a hole there, but I didn't even think about it. It was a snake den. So that evening they started to buzz. Boy, they buzzed all over. I was standing there holding that Chanunpa, and I heard a rattlesnake. So I was told that God created Heaven and Earth and everything. But I was thinking, "Oh, no, not that one." So I was standing there trying to pray and trying to listen to that rattle. At the same time, I was trying to give myself hell, trying not to chicken out. All this was going through my head at once.

Then a big snake came out of that hole. I knew he was coming to me. So I began to pray from my heart, from my spirit. So I started to navigate, recourse, and concentrate on who and why I was planted there. Then I got back on course. The vibration from that rattle on the snake started tingling in me. That tingling feeling started going up to my knees, then up to my body, then inside, then my teeth started clattering, and like that. The vibration went into my head, and my whole head started vibrating. Then there was a really powerful odor that came like a hot air. It felt like I was going into an oven. Boy, I was getting dizzy and perspiring all over. So I prayed and managed to pull through, but that snake kept coming.

Then he coiled around my ankle. So I should have took off before that. I should have took off when it was down there on the ground. Now I was frozen there. But I came there to die. This was vision quest. So I started thinking that maybe this is a good day to see my grandma. "Oh, when he bites me, I'll be dead in half an hour." I was thinking like that. At the same time I was still trying to give myself a little bit of encouragement. "Okay, Black Elk, are you going to chicken out or are you going to stay?" So all this was going through me. Your brain can work many ways in your head. So standing there holding the Chanunpa, I began to pray again. Finally I got it straight. I reaffirmed, rededicated myself. That spook went away.

Next thing that happened is that rattlesnake started crawling up my leg. He just coiled around it and started coming up. He crawled up my leg and coiled around my waist. "Oh, oh, it was a little better when he was down there around my ankle. I should have kicked it, or like that." I was thinking that way. But now he was around my waist, and I had a funny feeling. So I began to pray again.

When I got rid of that feeling, he started crawling again. He started crawling up and coiling around my neck. So it was a little better when he was around my waist. Now he's around my neck. Then he started tightening up, and it began to choke me. Sometimes his head would slide right in front of my face, and he would open his mouth. That tongue was whipping out, and there was a hot air blowing in my face. That gave me a spooky feeling. When he opened his mouth those fangs just swung out like that, like a pocket knife. Boy, that is going to make you think!

So I prayed again. I tried to get rid of it. "God created Heaven and Earth and everything. Hey, not this one!" I was trying to come in like that. I tried to pray again. Kept praying. I said, "Chanunpa is sacred. Chanunpa is sacred. Chanunpa is sacred." I couldn't stop. Then he started crawling down my arm. He coiled around my wrist and that Chanunpa. So I started thinking again. "How can that Chanunpa be sacred if some creature like this comes and coils around it? I can't throw it away because he's partly coiled around my wrist." So he was holding my wrist and Chanunpa together like that.

So I prayed again. "The Chanunpa is sacred." Now I was told when the Chanunpa is sacred, so, oh, oh, it's a warning. I thought I had the cure-all medicine right there in my hand. But it's not that way. It's a warning. So I stopped saying that the Chanunpa is sacred, and I began to pray to that Chanunpa. "Oh, Chanunpa, we always call you sacred."

Then there was a voice that came through that Chanunpa. It said, "Everybody calls me Chanunpa, but nobody ever says thank you to me. Nobody ever thanked me."

So right away I said, "Hey, thank you, Chanunpa, because that wisdom and knowledge and power is in you. Tunkashila carved this Chanunpa and gave it to us. So the 'In God We Trust' is in our hands. So now, the Chanunpa, I plead to you that you are sacred and all things that are around are sacred. You are the Creator, so you are sacred."

I prayed four times. Then I felt comfortable, you know. It felt like a hand, a human hand, touching me and giving me that comfort, like "Oh, good. Oh, thank you."

When I finished praying, that snake started sliding down, and, all of a sudden, there was a man standing in front of me wearing a robe. He said, "Ho, *hokshila.*" He called me "boy." Then he said, "You know you talk to me. There are four ways of life. There's a Black Nation, Red Nation, Yellow Nation, and the White Nation. These are four ways of life. You talk here like if they were in the palm of your hand." So he spoke to me like there were four divisions in the palm of your hand.

Then he said, "But now you are here, and you are really brave. You're courageous. And you are intelligent. You are smart. In fact, you speak two languages. You understand all this language. You are alert. You are aware of everything. You are quick to understand."

I thought he was bragging about me. So now I'm trying to figure out why he's trying to say all those things about me.

"Now," he said, "that patience is sitting on the tip of your tongue. The powers of the Four Winds, they are coming from all directions. Now they are going to give you that patience."

That's what he said to me. So I started trying to figure out what he meant. I was trying to figure out what "patience" meant.

Then he said, "I am here to tell you that these four divisions of people hold me as the most hated creature. These people think that I am the ugliest creature in the world. Yet Tunkashila gave me the power to protect this altar, this universe."

I said, "Oh, thank you." I got it. I earned that feat. The power of wisdom and knowledge was bundled and tied within me. So

I was equipped to understand the power of Tunkashila and the power of Grandmother the Earth.

Then he mentioned about those stone-people. So I started to pray, and the stone-people came. They came from above and sat around me. They all growled at me. So I thought that they were going to have a big feast. Those kind of thoughts started going through me again. I was scared, so I prayed again. Then that fear went away.

When I prayed, the stone-man came and said, "We sit here patiently. Tunkashila placed us here. We are stone-people. We sit here and watch and listen and know and feel everything that is around us. We sit here patiently watching. The reason these stone-people come here growling at you is because you mentioned that the elders and little ones are cold, hungry, sick, suffering, and dying. That is why the stone-people are growling. Some of those kids are in rags, and some are barefooted. Some are hungry. Some are sick and suffering pain and death. That is why the stone-people come around you and growl. They growl at the cause of this."

So then I understood why those stone-people were all growling. They were not growling at me but at the causes for all the suffering around us.

Then he said, "There are times that we roll and we walk and we also fly. But there will be a time that we are going to roll back and forth [have earthquakes]. We will tilt back and forth. Then tall buildings will tumble down, and countless people will vanish. Those people on the outside [of the buildings] will see this when we show that power. When that happens, those people on the outside, they will say, 'Oh, my God! Oh, my God!' But they are not praying to me. All they are really saying is, 'All my gold! All my gold!' " That's what he said.

Then he said, "The whole universe is a rock. It's an earth. The whole Earth is our eyes and hearing and sense of smell and taste and feeling. I gave the two-leggeds one drop of knowledge, and Tunkashila gave them one drop of wisdom and one drop of power and one drop of talent or gift. But man took that and used it to twist his own mind."

So these were things that I was told there. It was really good that I managed to pull through and was able to understand what was said. So it was really good to pray there. Then the medicine man came—the real one, the real McCoy, the real stuff, the real thing. That was the whole purpose for me going there. So now my prayers were answered. Now somebody was around my foot. Right under my foot he touched me and kind of pushed on the bottom of my foot. So I started to pray again. Those little thoughts started coming through me. I thought there might be a hole there and that a snake was going to come out and yell. "Maybe he's going to grab my foot and bite it." Those kinds of thoughts were going through me. So I tried to shake those off. I tried to pray again. And here, when I pointed that Chanunpa down to the earth and looked down, I saw like a shadow. There was a light that came from someplace, and I saw a shadow. At first I thought it was my shadow. Then I lifted the Chanunpa and pointed it upwards. While I was praying, my mind's eye caught this shadow. If this was my shadow, my head should be over there, and my arms and shoulders should be attached to my feet. But it wasn't that way. The head was over here, and the shoulders and arms were the other way.

So I started to pray again. Then I pointed the Chanunpa again down below to the earth. When I looked down this time, there was a man standing in the earth. There was a light there. It was solid earth, but he was walking around inside there. He came over, and, hey, he was poking at my feet. So talk about the medicine man, there he was poking at my feet. So I looked. So he went off into the dark, and then he came running. It was like he was taking a running start. He ran out of there and came onto the surface. So he stood on the level, ground surface.

Then he came up to me and said, "That Chanunpa you hold is very sacred. I'm a spirit. I was here, and the earth grew around me. I'm also from the fire. I'm also from the earth, from the rock. I'm also from the *wato,* the 'green.' I'm also from the water." That's what he said.

So I said, "Tunkashila, the fire, the rock, the water, and the green, these people [peyote] here are elected and appointed as chief among the cactus family. I come to visit you. I come to see you. So have pity on me and help my people. You are so merciful that you show yourself and speak to me through this Chanunpa. You honor me that way. Thank you." I was talking to the spirit like that.

Then the medicine man said [speaking of the Peyote religion], "You talk about this fire. People come here. These people make man-made laws. They say that man-made laws are the authority or the power. So man goes there, and he thinks that man-made laws are the power. So they bring a piece of paper [membership document] here. When I appear, they walk backwards and take off. Now those papers they have, they take that fire and make little fireplaces [peyote meetings] all the way around me. Those groups of people sit around the fire. Each one has a piece of paper. Those laws, rules, and regulations are written on paper, but those were all designed out of hatred and jealousy. So it's the same as though they were trying to tie my hands together. So there will be a time again that I will be back with this Chanunpa. I will be back again."

So as of now this cactus medicine is like joining a church [Native American Church] again. It's the same, like Christianity. They have Catholic, Episcopal, Presbyterian, and 285 labels all the way around. They put labels on Jesus. I think he was a good Joe, but they put labels all around him. So it's the same way. It's the same way with tobacco; they put brand names all the way around. So people believe in those brands, those labels. It's the same way with this medicine [peyote]; they put labels all the way around, see? It's organization.

Then he said, "Now this group of people, each sits around these fireplaces. They are connected. The four sicknesses that you mentioned to me, like cancer, polio, tuberculosis, and heart disease, they come from four man scratches on this earth."

He used the word *scratch.* Then he held out his hand and scratched four lines in the sand with his hand.

Then he said, "Because man is scratching the earth, that is where the sickness comes from. So you are going to go above, under, and around." That's what he said.

So he was, like, explaining it. You have to take it piece by piece. You have to understand what this *scratch* means. It's like when you are moving that earth to get to that coal. You call it strip mining. That's one of them. Then there is the poking a hole in the ground [drilling for gas/oil]. That's one of them. It goes like that. So that is where all the sickness comes from. It comes from mining uranium and coal and from the acid rain. So ten years from now all the acid rain that falls back to earth from burning tons of coal will be the equivalent destruction of a ten- to fifty-megaton bomb.

So when the spirit comes and talks, sometimes I'm afraid. I'm scared. So I really pray hard, because he could come in and explain things like this. I think this is science, and people should really know what they are doing. When they take uranium, they should know what to do with the residues. Or they should pray and ask permission from Tunkashila for what they are going to do with these residues. Then the spirit could tell them what to do with it. They could use some other source instead of just throwing it away. But they are eager to make more money, fast money. That's all. They want money now, today. So what will be the effect on our grandchildren ten years from now? But those people don't realize that way. So I want to tell you about this sacred way. That's how I was educated in this way. But, on the other hand, I'm not educated, see? I don't know how to push pencils or punch keys. I can't speak English. So it's really hard for me.

CHAPTER 10

Lost Horses and Souls

When the BIA people came to the reservation, they wanted to register all of the Indians. But they had a really hard time with our names. To us, a name told something about that person. So people's names were full of meaning to us. Of course, they could not understand our names when they were spoken in Lakota, but even when it was translated into English it was still too much for them to deal with. But they had to identify us, so they branded us with those names from the Bible in order to register us—okay, your name is Isaac; okay, your name is John; okay, your name is Mary; and like that. That's the way they wrote it down. So we got branded that way.

I'll tell you a funny story about the name given one of my uncles. His name was Rings-a-cowbell. When the Christian people would come around they would ask, "Where's Rings-a-cowbell?" I think they sort of liked that name. But they had a funny idea about how we got those names. Somebody wrote a book that said that when an Indian woman gave birth to a child, the first object she saw, she named her child after that. If she saw an eagle, she would name the child "Eagle," or if she saw a buffalo she would name the child "Buffalo," and like that. Well, those buffaloes are gone, and the eagle is becoming extinct. Now it would be funny if that tradition was still carried on today, because the first thing she is going to see might be a color TV or a Budweiser or a Cadillac. Maybe she'd see a pumpkin at Halloween or a Santa Claus. So she might even see a rabbit laying colored eggs. (It's funny how those eggs never hatch.) Anyway, back to my uncle's name.

My uncle, he had a girlfriend, and they liked to go powwow—dance, beat the drum, dance. But he was married to this other woman, and she was more Christian. She had been converted, so she didn't believe in powwow and all that Indian stuff. Those "sweat-lodges" and altar ceremonies, they were run by devil worshipers. They were possessed by devils. She thought that way. So she would tell everyone not to go there. She would tell them not to eat those medicines either, because they were serpent food. So she would tell them to stay on this side and eat bread and wine over here. She would say, "If you're sick, then we have hospitals. You can go there and eat the right pills." So she was brought up that way. She didn't believe in our medicine powers. But my uncle, he believed in those powers.

So my uncle told this girl that they have a cow that always jumps out of the corral. Right next to the corral was a cornfield. So that cow liked to go over into the cornfield to feed. So my uncle put a cowbell around that cow so he could find her when she got out. Now he told this girl to take that cowbell and come to that cornfield when it was dark and ring that bell. That way he could tell his wife that the cow was out and that he had to go get her out of the cornfield.

So that day he was polishing his boots and trying on his new hat in front of the mirror. His wife said, "Thinking of going some place?"

He said, "Oh, no, I'm just airing out this outfit."

Then he hung his new hat and jacket by the door. That evening, after it got dark, he heard that cowbell ringing in the cornfield. He said, "Oh, that cow got out into the cornfield." So he grabbed his new hat and coat and ran out of the house yelling, "Heh! Heh! Heh!"

His girlfriend had come to the cornfield ringing that bell. When he ran out of the house, he opened the corral gate so the cow could go out and eat. Then that cow could get lost, and he could look for her the next day before someone butchered it. So he ran into the cornfield, grabbed the bell, grabbed his girlfriend, and ran through the cornfield. While he was running, he was shaking that cowbell and yelling, "Heh! Heh! Heh!" He started running faster and ringing that cowbell faster—double ring. At the end of the cornfield, he just threw that cowbell and took off with his girlfriend.

So he went to the dance and came back early in the morning. The cow was gone. So he went to look for her. That was just an excuse. He went to the neighbors, and he slept there all day. So later on people found out about this, and they began to talk. They would say, "Oh, you're a good singer," or "How's that girl you danced with?" So that's how the word got around. He was found out. So his whole name became: "Rings-a-cowbell-as-he-runs-through-the-cornfield-with-his-girlfriend-in-one-hand." That was his name. But it was too long to write, so they kept cutting it off. They kept cutting off parts of it and finally ended up with only "Rings-a-cowbell." When the Christian people found out about this, they said his name was a mortal sin. So they just shortened it to "Bell." That way some people might think his name was Church Bell or Liberty Bell. So that was my uncle's name.

One time a young man, a white boy, came, and he wanted to have a Chanunpa ceremony because he had lost three horses. He also lost his silver-mounted saddle, spurs, martingale, and bridle. Those had belonged to his grandfather, so they were a keepsake for him. But somebody came along with a loading chute for horses, so he took them away in a truck. He also took his grandfather's keepsakes. That boy didn't use them or anything like that. But they belonged to his grandfather, so he just valued them for a keepsake.

Anyway, when this guy was eleven years old he got pneumonia. His grandfather and grandmother were alive then. Down the creek a little ways there lived some old people, an Indian man, a medicine man. So they got acquainted, and they always helped each other. When the old man had a lodge ceremony, the white man would crawl in. They prayed together. So they always helped each other. So when that boy got sick it was winter. There was snow, heavy snow, and all the roads were blocked. There was no road there for cars, but probably a horse-drawn wagon could go there sometimes. Anyway, this time there was too much snow, so those horses couldn't pull the wagon through that snow. And it was a long way to the main highway. So it was impossible to get a doctor out there or to get that kid to the hospital. Then his grandfather remembered this Indian friend that lived up the creek. So he waded through that big snow to get to that Indian medicine. Then he brought that medicine man back. The medicine man told them they would need to have a lodge ceremony. But they were nowhere, and there was no lodge there. Well, there was a little chicken coop there, so they decided to use that for the lodge. They pulled out all those chickens and put them into the house. Then they covered that chicken coop. They built a snow shelter and built a fire there to heat up the stone-people. Then they hauled those hot stones into that chicken coop. Then the mother of that boy dragged him into the lodge. He was really sick. He had double pneumonia. His eyes were turned up, and he took little short breaths.

Then that old man running the ceremony called in the spirit. The spirit, the real medicine man, came in. So that Indian gave that boy some medicine. While he was being doctored, they were singing songs, short songs, in there. All of a sudden you could hear gargling. Like you take water and gargle. That sound was in there. This boy's lungs were full of fluid, and he was like drowning. That medicine pulled all that water out. You could hear it coming out. It went out. Then they fanned him. They gave him that pure oxygen. Then his lungs were clear. So he started breathing. He was conscious. They gave him water. So he drank water. Then he was healed. His lungs were cleaned out. So he walked out.

So that boy, after his grandfather died, he went to college. Later his mother and father died, so he inherited that land. He remembered that old man that had doctored him. He remembered that he had saved his life. He remembered those old people. He remembered what had happened. He remembered that bond, that prayer. So he respected the Chanunpa and the lodge. So he came over to us. He came over to the reservation in search of the lodge and the Chanunpa.

He started asking, "Is there anybody that's a medicine man, or is there any sweat-lodge, or any of that?"

So somebody told him, "Yeah. You go to Parmalee [South Dakota] and look for Black Elk. I think he's familiar with all that area. He could lead you."

So I was at my dad's place, and there was a pickup that drove up. I heard, "Somebody's here in a pickup." I never saw him before. So he came up to me and said, "Hi. Is your name Black Elk?"

"Yeah."

"My daddy told me the story [about my cure]. It's a long story, but I'll tell you. You'll get to know. I'll make this long story short . . . and I want to offer you a Sacred Pipe."

So when he finished that story, I told my dad. He said, "Yeah. That's good. So accept the Chanunpa. I'll give you that honor. You are going to act as interpreter. You are going to interpret for the spirit. Good." So I accepted that honor, that Chanunpa.

So we put him to work getting the altar ready. We itemized all the things we would need—tobacco, string, eagle feather, eagle plume, conch shell, wood, sacred foods, different colored robes in black, red, yellow, white, blue, and green. So he wrote it all down. Then he left. Later he came back. He brought six bolts of material, the whole thing, the whole bolt. Inside his pickup he had two halves of beef from the slaughter house. He had them hanging inside the pickup. He had a rack on it. Then the corn. He brought a case of corn. There were six gallon-cans of corn in that box. In another box there were six cans. They were gallons of fruit. And there was more. There was a box of Bull Durham tobacco in those little sacks. I think there were about two dozen in there. He brought six of those. And those spools of twine, you know, he brought six of those.

When my mom saw all of that she started to really laugh. She said, "Oh, no. We are not going to use all of that."

So he said, "Well, I just brought this for distribution among the people. So you take whatever you want. Take whatever you need."

So we only took a half yard each of those materials for the robes and enough to make those prayer ties. Then he wrote out a check for five hundred dollars to my dad. My dad said, "Ho. That's good."

Then the ceremony began. That boy was sitting behind the altar. He called me "Chief." When the spirit came in, this guy started nudging me. He thought that was an Indian spirit that came in. So he said, "You've been with this spirit all your life. But I'm a *wasichu.* I'm a white man. So he might not understand my English language."

So I said, "No. He's a spirit. He hears all languages. He'll hear you."

But that doubt was still there. So he said, "No. You'd better talk to him because he is an Indian spirit. So you'd better talk to him in Lakota."

So I said—I said it in Lakota—"Tunkashila, my white brother here said that you're a Lakota spirit. He's a white man. He speaks English, and you might not understand English. So he asked that I talk to you in Lakota. Whatever he needs, whatever you want to say to him, you can tell me, and I'll translate for him. He wants it that way. But I told him that you are spirit. You are sacred. You hear. You understand. Besides, you see much deeper how he feels, where he comes from, and all this. You know when he was born and why he's here and when he's going to die. You know everything."

So that spirit came closer. Then that spirit said, "I read his mind. I know the way he is thinking. That piece of wood and that piece of stone [Sacred Pipe] lying there is sacred. Tell him that."

So I interpreted that. So I told him that the spirit had read his mind. I told him that the spirit has said that he was thinking about that piece of wood and piece of stone because he had a college degree. So in that language it's just a piece of wood and a piece of stone with maybe a little green in there, like that. That is the way he was thinking.

Then I said, "He's a spirit. He's the one that gave you that language. If you believe that, then speak to him in that language he gave you. Then he'll answer you in the language he gave you. So that spirit is going to talk English."

So to my surprise this white boy said, "Gee, Tunkashila. I'm very sorry. I'm terribly sorry. I shouldn't have doubted this. It's

your medicine people that helped me. A long time ago, when I
was a boy, I was dying. You came, and you doctored me. You
made me well through this Indian friend of my grandfather. All
that I remember is that old Indian that rescued me. He gave me
my health back. So I owe my life to that old man. So that has
stayed with me all this time. That is the reason I came here. But
I don't know these sacred powers. So I came here because I need
your help. I lost three horses, and I lost my grandfather's saddle.
It's not for me to keep or use. But those horses, I paid a lot of
money for them. That saddle horse especially, that one horse, I
paid twenty thousand dollars for him. I want to keep those
horses. I don't want to work them every day. I just want to keep
them for harnessing to the wagon and just driving around. I want
to keep them for my kids. So that's the only reason I want those
horses back. Now a truck backed into the loading chute, and
somebody loaded up those horses and took them away. The
sheriff has been there, and even the FBI came there. All they
found was one little tire track. So they traced that tread pattern.
But there are thousands of tires with that brand that are sold in
this area. So there is no way to trace that truck down. As soon
as it drove onto the blacktop that trail ended. So they couldn't
find it."

So that spirit said, "Sing four songs. I'll backtrack for this
white boy. I'm going to backtrack for him."

So we started singing those songs. Then that spirit took off to
backtrack that truck. He went over to the house where that white
boy lived. There he picked up the trail and traced it. He even went
on that blacktop. There are thousands of those tires, the same
kind of tire, going over and over on that blacktop. But he traced
that track. During the last song he came back in.

He said, "Yeah. I found it. And I brought those things that you
wanted to keep from your grandfather. I brought them here and
laid them on the top of this roof. If you want, I could bring them
in."

So that white boy said, "Yes, Tunkashila. I want them in here.
Please bring them in."

So we sang a song. Then you could hear this rolling sound. It
sounded like gravel sliding down a chute. It was that sound. You

could hear the straps slapping and those spurs jingling. Then we heard this flop.

Then the spirit said, "After we leave here, when they finish this and turn the lights on, you go north by northeast. When you come to a blacktop, then you go straight north. Then you will come to a big junction. There you turn to the west and go to the fourth big town. When you go there, there will be a stockyard there. You go there. When you go there, you will see your horses there. So from there you know what to do."

Then that boy he said, "Oh, thank you. Thank you."

Then we finished the ceremony. When we turned on the lights, that saddle, spurs, and bridle were sitting by the altar. So how did the spirits bring them in? That's a mystery. But that made him really happy. After the ceremony, he got into his pickup. He went right away. Just around sunrise he got to Rapid City, South Dakota. So he went into the stockyard. He walked on the catwalks over the pens, and there he saw his horses. But it was too early, and no one was in the stockyard. So he walked across the street to an open café and got a cup of coffee. When the time came, somebody opened the doors to the stockyard. So he went there and told them that those horses in there were his horses. Then he called the sheriff. From there the investigation was easy. So after an hour, or an hour and a half, they tracked down that man that stole those horses. So they caught him. So he loaded his horses and started racing back.

He came back to our place around noon. He said, "I want to put up a thank-you ceremony."

So we said that would be good. So he started the fire—put the rocks on, stacked the wood around, prayed, and lit it. My mom and my sisters started making the robes and prayer ties. They started cooking the food. Then we performed that ceremony.

After that thank-you ceremony he said, "Now don't ever hesitate. Whenever you guys need help, just call me. I'd like to be a part of it."

So when we have those desperate times, we call him. He says, "Don't worry. I'll be there. You wait for me." Then he brings food. He brings chickens, frozen meat, or a whole cow in a pickup. So my grandpa, grandma, dad, and mom, they all prayed for him. The spirit always returns those prayers. So his cattle raising increased. All the other ranchers kept losing cattle, but his were strong and in good health. The spirit helped him. He, his wife, and children, they are in good health. So things happen that way. So when we send a voice to Tunkashila, that prayer is not just temporary for a month. It's not that way. It goes from generation to generation.

So my grandfathers, they were really smart people. Those old people were really different. They didn't think like these Christian people. According to the Christian people over here, if you commit suicide you condemn your own spirit. Then your spirit belongs to the devil. You can't go to Heaven. But you could kill a man, and God will forgive you. You could still go through the Pearly Gates. But if you kill yourself, then you go straight to hell. But this Chanunpa saves souls. Tunkashila is the real, true amnesty. So we pray to Tunkashila. That person made one mistake. That person didn't realize what he was doing. So we ask Tunkashila to forgive that man who took his life. Then Tunkashila will forgive that man and bring his spirit back to him.

I have done that before. I had three nephews commit suicide right in the same jail. It happened month after month after month. Like one of my nephews, his sister was my niece. They were Christian people. So when they brought the remains of her brother into her house, she was crying. And the father, the priest, went there. He told her that if somebody takes their life, then that spirit belongs to the devil. God cannot forgive it. So that just added more sorrows for her—losing her brother, then somebody comes and condemns his spirit. So it's like a double death. So that made my niece nearly lose her mind. So I prayed for her.

So we put up a lodge for my nephew. We put the robes and the food there and went in. Then my niece came in. We started to pray to the Four Directions. Then a spirit came in. He asked, "What do you want?"

So I said, "Oh, Tunkashila, my nephew took his own life. I want to know what happened. I want to know where his spirit is. I want his spirit to come here. I want to know."

Then they sang four songs. The spirit went up and went [to the] Four Directions. They sang for a long time. Then that spirit returned and brought my nephew in. As he was coming, he was crying.

When he came in, he said, "Uncle, when I was wearing my robe [in my body] I should have listened to you. But I kept boozing, taking drugs, and doing all that stuff. I was doing destructive things. For that, I was the most hated guy. I terrorized my father, mother, sister, sons, daughters, nephews, nieces, all my relatives. For that, I was not wanted. I got thrown in jail. When I came back, I didn't have any place to go. All I had were the clothes I wore. I had no place to lie down and rest. Everywhere I went they would call the police. They'd cuss me up. Some people even kicked me, knocked me down, knocked me out, beat me up, because I made it that way for myself.

"I should have listened to you when you talked about the Chanunpa. So I went and thought about what all was happening to me. I decided I might as well resign. I decided to blank everything out—to forget everything. So I took that clothes hanger, and I went to that shack. I poked it through those cracks. I made a loop out of that clothes hanger and put it around my neck. Then I had a little gallon can. So I stood on it and put that loop around my neck and kicked that can."

So that's what he did. His neck stretched out real long. He broke his neck. So his toes and knees were kind of buckled. And he hung there for days until somebody found him.

So when my nephew came into the lodge, he told me everything that went through his mind until the very end. Then he said, "Then, when I hanged myself, it was like taking off your coat and hanging it on a clothes rack. My robe was hanging there, and I was still standing beside it. Then I looked around, and I could see the wonders of the Great Spirit. I could see the wonders of Grandmother, the Earth. When the black light approached me, I could see all these creatures around me. That scared me. I didn't know where to go. I tried to call, but no one answered. I went to those places where they have churches. I went inside those churches, in and around those churches. But it was empty and cold. I had a cold feeling. Emptiness. There was nobody.

"There were people that went there. I tried to talk to them. I tried to tell them to pray for me. But these people never saw me.

They just ignored me. They just kept walking back and forth. So I was scared. Like all this town made a lot of noises, but they were empty noises. But through this Chanunpa, I heard loud and clear. I heard that eagle-bone whistle. That sound you made was so beautiful. I heard it four times. Then the powers started coming all around me. They herded me and brought me here. As I was coming, that whistle got louder and louder. Then I could see you people sitting in the lodge. I saw your tears. You prayed for me. You called me back. That bond of love came from here. Even for all the things I did, you people didn't condemn me. Instead, with your love, you called me back. That Chanunpa has a power."

So we brought him back. He was crying. He went the wrong way—intentionally and knowingly he went the wrong way. He knew it, but he went anyway. So I prayed for him. Then the powers of the Four Winds brought my brother and his wife. This boy was my brother's son. So in the Lakota way, he was my son. So they brought his father and mother to greet him. So I gave him the tobacco ties and the sacred foods—the water, the corn, the berries and meat. He took that scent, that flavor, and digested it. Then he stopped crying. He felt good. He felt happy. Then he thanked me.

"Dad, uncle, I love you. Thank you very much. Thank you for bringing my father and mother to greet me."

So when he turned around, I told him that I had made a little pouch to take with him. So he took the pouch and went around. His father and mother came to the altar. He greeted them. They were both crying. They were happy to see their son. But that was not the way they wanted to see him, so they cried. And like the old saying, the prodigal child came home, and they welcomed him with opened arms. They sort of celebrated, you know, because he had been lost, but now he came home. He was dead, but he came home.

So the father and mother hugged their son. Then they said it was time to go back to the spiritual camp. So the powers of the Four Winds came and took them there. They took his father, mother, and him to the spiritual camp. And Tunkashila and Grandmother, they forgave him. They wiped his tears and set him free. This Chanunpa could do that. It's sacred. So I went inside these powers. I had to go through these powers to get to the firsthand information. So I learned a lot from this Chanunpa.

I have seen these things happen. These powers can do unbelievable things. They could find missing persons. Even if they are dead, they could bring them back. They could tell you when they died. They could tell you who killed them. They could tell you if there was foul play. I could perform those ceremonies, but if I found someone dead, then someone is going to get arrested. So they are going to ask who told them that. So then they'll say it was Black Elk. Then it's, "Who told you?"

"Well, it was the spirit."

"What spirit?"

So it would be going like that. But we have performed ceremonies like that.

Like one time they brought a Chanunpa to my dad and mom. My cousin was there. So my dad said, "Cousin, they brought a Chanunpa. If you want to take it, if you want to accept it, you go ahead. If you take it, cousin, I'll go with you."

Those people that came there were desperate. So they went ahead and took it. Then we smoked it together. So then they asked what was the purpose of this Chanunpa presentation. So those people explained. They had lost their boy. He was about eleven years old. He had fallen in the Missouri River and had been gone for about two weeks now. They had divers come there in boats. They had hooks and dragnets and had used everything for two weeks. But that river was so fast and so deep that they couldn't find that boy.

So they were Christian people. They were Indians like us, but they were converts. They didn't believe in the Chanunpa. But now they had to. Somebody had told them that the only way they were going to find their son was to go to a medicine man, a Chanunpa man. If they offered a Chanunpa, then they will help you find him. But they didn't know where to go. So some people told them, "You have to get a Chanunpa and fill the Chanunpa and go west. You might find somebody. If you go there, well, maybe they will help you. They might give you instructions. You might put up an altar or go into the sweat-lodge. They might direct you. You might get help. It may be possible that they will do it, or maybe they won't. At least if you go, you will find out if they could do it or not. Otherwise, your boy will be gone forever. You'll never see him. The fish will eat him up, or he'll just go to the bottom and deteriorate. If you don't go, you might as well bury him in the water." There was a lot of talk going on like that.

So that was the reason those people came there with the Chanunpa. So we said, "Okay. Let's go." So we went into the lodge, and we wiped [ritually cleansed] ourselves. Then we went over to their house. People came in there and sat down. The sheriff was there also. Then that father and mother came in. So I sat there and acted as interpreter for the spirit. So we started, and the spirit came in.

We prayed to him, "Tunkashila, please find us a helper. Find somebody or something that will help us recover the remains of that little boy. His parents have an aching heart. There is a pain in their hearts. They want to find their flesh that has gone under the water."

Then we sang a song, and a beaver spirit came in. He walked around. He was shaking, and water sprinkled all over us. Then he asked us what we wanted. So we said, "There is a boy that lost his life in the water. Maybe you could go and help us locate him. His father and mother have tears of sadness. They want to know at least if their son is dead. At least they want to recover the remains. That's what they want."

So the beaver said, "Oh, sing four songs. I'm going to leave. If I don't return by the fourth song, then you will have to find another helper." So we sang four songs. Everybody prayed. On the fourth song, he came back in. He shook that water off, and you could see his water tracks in there. Then he said, "Yes, I found him. He was buried underneath a stump in the sand. So I dug him out. There is a curve over there and like a wall. There is a tree growing there, so the roots stick out of that wall. So I took him there, and I hung him over those roots. Tomorrow you go over to that river. You go there with the Chanunpa. Then you walk along that river. When you hear me, you come in that direction. You pray and walk in that direction. You come to the edge of the water. You look down. You stand there and look until you see the remains there. Then you signal, and they will come help you to pick him up." So we thanked him, and he left.

The next day we went over there. We walked along [the river], and then we heard that sound—swoosh—like that. So we turned around and headed in the direction of that sound. We prayed. We walked straight to the edge and looked down. So we were standing there watching. Pretty soon we saw him. His arm was hanging over that tree root, just below the water. So the sheriff was there, and he ran back to his radio. Pretty soon the boats came. They were about a mile and a half away. When they got there, some people dove into the water and pulled him into the boat. Then they went back.

So we went back and went to the lodge. His father and mother were there. They smoked that Chanunpa. Then they went to that place where the boats landed. They were hosing that boy down, washing off all that sand and mud. So the father and mother identified him. "Yes. That's him."

So we have found people that way. But it's sacred. So we have to go to the lodge for three nights to go all the way through. Then at the end we have to wipe ourselves, because these people don't know the sacred ways. So we do that for ourselves, and we get a lot of help. So when we finished helping those people find their little boy, we wiped [ritually cleansed] ourselves, said thank you, and left. After that, a lot of people started coming in. So there were a lot of people coming back to the Chanunpa. It was really unbelievable how this Chanunpa way helped that family to find their boy's remains. But that also helped many people to really understand the Chanunpa and to understand that the Earth People way of life is real. It's not just devil worship or possession by demons. It not that way. It's sacred.

CHAPTER 11

The Power of Iktomi

Don't think of me as a superman. I'm just a little guy. I'm just like you or anybody else. So my heart is made out of flesh too. I wish my heart was made out of gold or a piece of stone, but I'm not that way. So there are times I get weak, too. Sometimes all those psychological burdens that I have to pack on my back are bearing down on me. Then people come and help me to lift up. The spirit comes, and it just blows away. Then I feel good. I take a breather. Then I know where I came from. I know I am part of the spirit. I'm part of the spark. I'm part of the electrical. I'm part of the atom. So I know that. Then that fire became a rock. So I became a part of the dirt. And I became part of the water, because I drink water. Also, I'm part of the green. I'm just like a little plant. Like there is a plant here, and you pour water on it. So I drink water.

But over here it's really hard to be in this other philosophy [Western civilization]. It's really hard. When you are born, you have to pay to be born. Then if you're sick, whether this medical science cures you or kills you, you still have to pay. And when you die, you still have to pay to be buried. So from birth to death you have to pay. You have to pay for everything.

In the Earth People philosophy I'm not even worth being put in a casket. So I prayed to Tunkashila, "Tunkashila, have mercy on me. Please take me. Take my robe with you. I give you my robe, and I dedicate and commit my spirit into your sacred hands."

And he said, "That will be so."

So that really made me feel good. So when I die, the spirit, the power, will come, and they will take me to the West. They will lay my robe there, and then I will be in spirit. But I'll be able to come back and communicate with you. So this is going to be the first time in world history that there will be no burial, because the spirit will take my robe. So there will be nothing there to put in that casket. So I was really glad that I was able to obtain that power. I don't want to be buried. I want to live with my people. So when the spirit came, that was my request. So it is good. I feel good. So I feel safe on both sides now.

So I'm totally different. No wonder they call me strange. So it's really funny. We are strange, yet we are a part of Tunkashila. Like when I went to the World Court in Geneva, all those law-making people came together, and they ended up not knowing what was legal and what was not legal. So they asked me if I knew. So I laughed, and I said, "What is not legal is me." But there is a universal law, and those people really didn't understand about that law. So speaking from the universe of mind, there is a universal law. There is Tunkashila and Grandmother; she is the supreme law of the land. And the law in itself is understanding, and that spells love. So the law in itself is Tunkashila, and the love that you understand is your Mother. We are all part of the Mother. We all came from a woman, see? So if I explain all of this, it is going to take you eight years before you really understand what I am saying. So you can't learn about these powers in just a few days.

But you know, it's kind of funny that way. I enjoy the job I have. It makes me feel like a little somebody. It's an honor for me to say something good. So it may seem like it's me saying it, but it isn't. I'm just a little instrument. I'm just one of those little prayer ties. So that's good. I enjoy helping people. If somebody falls, we never leave him lie there and go on. We always stop and, at least, raise him up or help him to stand. We help him walk until he gets on his feet again. Now I'm standing on the top of the mountain. I can see the [Earth People] life over here on this side and the destruction [via industrialization] over there on the other side. So I say, "Hey, this way. This way. Hey, over here. Life over here." So that is my way. My way is the Chanunpa way. My way is health and help. So we help a lot of people with this Chanunpa.

Like one time there was this little boy. He was born normal, but in just a few months he couldn't drink, and he couldn't cry. Later on, he couldn't sit up, and he couldn't walk. So he was this way for about four years. He was in the hospital for four years. And the doctors, they didn't know what was wrong with this kid. They had to stick a tube down his throat and pour food in there. He would chew on crackers, but he couldn't swallow them. They just spilled from the corner of his mouth. So he kind of cried when he was trying to eat. Tears would come down. So his father, mother, relatives, everybody felt bad. They wanted to do something, but what could they do?

So we talked to the doctor, but the medical staff there wouldn't listen. They were law-abiding citizens, so they had to obey all those rules and regulations. They agreed with me, but they couldn't change those laws. So they had to follow that way. Then they thought that maybe they could ask that board of directors, because there is this board over their heads. So they wanted to ask permission from that board of directors that I be allowed to give that boy medicine. I told them that it was going to be difficult for them to understand what I did and to make a report on that.

Anyway, this doctor talked to the board, and, finally, they granted his request. It only took him twenty-four hours to get the okay. So we set a time and date for the healing ceremony. That boy was in the Fitzsimmons Army Medical Center in Denver. It's a big hospital, and that boy was on the fourth floor there. So we went there to the fourth floor. This doctor was there, and there was a registered nurse there also sitting on a chair. He said that the nurse was going to be an assistant because she was interested. She wanted to know about this healing ceremony, and she wanted to see it for herself.

So she told us, "I'm sick and tired of this routine we have to follow around here. I've seen countless little kids, not just this one, but thousands of them suffer. There are countless people out there, little people, even adults that are suffering. And we can't do anything for them. So at least this one time, I think that some progress will be made here."

So that was good. So we got an isolation ward there. We had to block off all the windows there with black plastic and duct tape, so that the ceremony could be conducted in the black light. On the floor under the doorway, there was a little light coming in through there. So we taped that shut also. In the meantime, there were all these staff people out there in the hallway moving those other patients. They were taking all the patients from that wing, so they wouldn't be affected by this noise-maker [drum] we brought there. They told them that there were going to be some wild Indians there and that they would be banging on a drum. So there was going to be a lot of noise there, so, if you wish, we'll move you.

Then a lot of them told the doctor, "No. We don't want to move. We want to stay. We want to hear the Indians."

So they didn't want to move. So they gave us two hours for that ceremony. We had to do it between seven P.M. and nine P.M. So after nine o'clock, everybody should be in bed asleep. Some of those people there were in pain. So they give them those pain pills, and then they should sleep or rest. So we can't be disturbing them that way.

But these patients were asked before we started, and they didn't want to move. They'd rather stay. Some of them were bed patients, some were in wheelchairs, and some had IVs in their foot or arm. The doctor would bring that IV in there on little wheels with that little jar hanging on there. Anyway, that was taken care of. So, finally, we went into that isolation ward, and we displayed the altar. That little boy was there in a crib. There was an oxygen bottle there and lots of little gadgets with lights. So we had to tape over every one of those little lights with electrical tape. We turned the lights off. We tested. There were no lights, just pitch black.

So we began. We explained to the doctor and the registered nurse what was going to take place, what was to be expected there. Then we sang those songs—honoring song, the Four Winds and callings songs. About that time we heard a thunder—boom—like that. And then there was a flash of light, and somebody came in. It was like a ghost. You know, at Halloween you see a sheet with arms out. It was not exactly like that, but there was a glow of light there. It was shaped like a man. It came in and came to the altar.

He said, "Well, what's the purpose of calling me?"

So I answered his question, "Tunkashila, we have a little boy here. There is something wrong with him. Nobody knows what it is. He's been suffering here for many years. So we ask that you help us to help this little boy."

So he went over to that little boy. The nurse was standing by the crib, and the doctor was sitting behind the altar. That spirit went over there, and then he came back. He told us what was wrong with that little boy. He talked about the brain and two nerves that branch out right at the neck. The unknown power had taken a spider web and tied a knot around one of those nerves. Right at the throat there was another knot tied there. So there are some muscles there in a ring. They contract when you swallow or use your vocal cords. It was tied there, so there were no contractions or release. Where it was tied, it affected the power of the whole system. That's why that little boy couldn't sit up or fall backwards. So he was just like a little baby, but here he was five years old. So wherever he lay, that's where he stayed. So you would have to move him, roll him around, put him back on his side, and all that. When the mealtime came, they would stick that tube down his throat and have to pour milk in there down to his stomach. Then he would go to sleep, like that.

At the same time, they had done everything. They took X rays and had all this research going on, but they didn't know what was wrong with him. But here this spirit came in, and right away he diagnosed what was wrong. Then that spirit revealed to us the instructions for healing this little boy. He told us we would have to call a spider spirit in, an *iktomi*. Right away we sang that *iktomi* calling song. So that red spider, he came in. He's the leader of all the spiders. So the leader came in.

Then he asks, "What do you want?"

So I answered him, "Well, some unknown power used your web to tie up this little kid. So he's been suffering. The medical science, they have no answer, because they don't know what is the matter with him. They can't see this web with their micro-scopes. That X ray just goes right through there, and it doesn't tell them where the pain is. It doesn't tell them anything. That machine doesn't see this web. After many years of research, they could see those little grooves wrapped around the nerve. So they take a little surgical knife and cut it. But once they cut the nerve, it injures the nerve. So they don't have a knife small enough to cut that web. They don't have any little tiny hand tweezers that can break it."

So that red spider understood what I said. Then we sang a song. So he goes over to that little boy, and he untangles that web around his throat. He does it, just like that. He knows how because that's his web. So he could climb it. He knows about that because that is a part of him. That's part of his ingenuity.

Then he came back and said, "I took that web off. So that boy is going to educate his muscles now, and he is going to make sounds. So you are going to hear his voice now for the first time."

By that time, that kid had started moving around. You never heard him talk or cry. But now there was a sound coming out of him—awwwk, awwwk—like that. So he didn't know how to make sounds. So he was just making a sound like that. He was glad just to hear his own voice. So he kept doing that—awwwk, awwwk, awwwk. Each time it was getting louder and louder and louder. Or he would do it long or go up in that sound. So he started going high pitch, then low pitch, then medium pitch, and like that. He kept moving that same sound around.

Then the spirit said, "So it's not going to be hard to feed him now. So let him eat and drink what he wants. He'll stop by himself. So he could educate his muscles now. So that's all. That's it."

So we thanked him, "Oh, thank you. Thank you." So we sang the pipe song. In there we sing, "Oh, Tunkashila. The tobacco ties and the robes, we give you these. So touch them or take them."

So that spider said, "Yes. I will take them."

So I said, "Yeah, good. Go with you. I thank you for coming and helping our little one here. We give you these offerings. And here's some food. I thank you."

So he took that food and ties and robes. Then he said, "I am going to take them and go." Then we sang the departing song, and that *iktomi* spirit left.

So that nurse said, "Oh, doctor. I want to turn the lights on." And that kid, he's screaming, making all kinds of sounds. And that little crib started moving. And the nurse is talking to that little boy. So when we turned on the lights, that little kid was standing up. Then they gave him some milk in a cup. Normally, he couldn't drink out of a cup. But he took that cup and started drinking and drinking. He really enjoyed that. Then he asked for more. But that nurse was a little fearful, "No, honey, I think we had better take it easy." But he keeps going. He still feels really good. Tears are coming down, and he's really happy. He's licking his lips and asking for more, more, more, and like that.

So that registered nurse got scared. She thought that he was going to overload his stomach, and it might break. That's what she was scared of. Before that she had only given him four or eight ounces every so many hours apart. But here this kid was drinking and drinking and drinking. Now what the spirit had said came true. It became reality. So they gave him crackers and baby food and like that. He can't really eat, you know. But he ate and ate and drank and ate and ate and ate, like that. We gave him soup, and we gave him more to drink. So that nurse was getting more scared. Anyway, he kept going and going. Finally, he stopped.

Then he rolled over and grabbed his toes. He rocked back and forth. Then he got up.

So I said, "Put him on the floor. He'll run around."

So they took him out of that crib. He got up on the couch, and he started walking around. He was balancing himself and laughing and laughing. He was making that same sound—awwwk, awwwk—and laughing at the same time. So he had to learn how to laugh. So he was walking back and forth there. He would reach and grab, then turn around or start rocking again. He would put his head down and touch his toes. Then roll over, flip over, or walk all around. He kept going on like that. So we were just sitting there watching him.

One thing I forgot to tell you. When we turned on those lights, that sacred food, the robes, and the tobacco ties, they were all gone. So that spirit took those offerings with him. So that doctor got real curious.

"How did he take all that stuff through the wall? How did he do that?"

When we looked at the altar, the only thing left were those little sticks there that we tied those robes to. So the doctor started to write all this down. He was standing there with his little notebook scratching away. Then he stopped and played with that kid. That nurse was playing with him also. So it was a really good feeling there.

So now the problem comes. This doctor is taking notes, and he is going to have to write that report. That's where the problem begins! Well, he couldn't report that first he saw us close the door, then we sang some songs, then a ghost came in, and like that, you know. That's really hard for a doctor to write that. Then the ghost came over and told us that the nerve had been tied with a spider web. Now that's even harder! Then those rings, those circles were really tight around his throat, so we called a spider in, and a red spider came in. Then that spider ran over there, and he untied that web. So how is he going to make a report to the medical science?

So he said, "I don't know how I'm going to report this. I don't know whether they will believe this or not. I don't know what to put down. I don't know. Well, I'll make a separate report over here."

So he just wrote it all down like it happened—then the spider took off, then the boy was making sounds, then they fed him, and he ate and ate, then he was walking around, doing somersaults, and all this.

So after that we open the door, and all those patients, they were standing there in the hallway. Some of them had never been up before. They would have to crank them up in bed to make them sit in the sitting position. So the spirit did that. When they heard that drum, that spirit came in, and he also told us, "I see all these people lying here. I will go over there, and I will fan them. I will give them a little air, pure oxygen. So they will sniff that, and the water will digest in their system. It will remove those poisons."

So here's all these people now in the hallway. Some of them are pushing their IVs around on those little wheels, but those IVs don't get rid of that bacteria. But here this spirit had given them water, and it removed that poison, it neutralized those bacteria in there. Some of those people, their muscles were not educated. They would send that little command wave from their brain to wave or open their arms, but their muscles couldn't respond. Their hands and feet wouldn't respond. And that little memory box in there was deteriorated, so they could hardly remember anything. It sort of got rusted, like their little computer chip got kind of worn out. So they can't remember anything.

So anyway, all these people were out there in the hallway. Some of the staff were saying to them, "Hey, you're supposed to be in bed. What are you doing out here?" It was going on like that. And here others, "Oh, I forgot my cane," or, "Oh, I forgot my wheelchair."

So everybody forgot that they were sick. Anyway, those people that worked there kept saying, "Okay, everybody get back. Crawl back in your bed. Get. Get going." They kept talking like that to them. So everybody started scrambling back to their little isolated rooms. But they felt better.

So we came out of the room with that little kid. The doctor and the nurse took him down below to the other doctors. He walked around.

So they started asking, "What did you do to him? How did you make him this way?"

So he said, "Well, I didn't do it. It's those dumb Indians that came. They brought a piece of wood and a piece of stone. They said something, and something came in. It diagnosed the problem and removed the cause. And this little guy is walking around. He makes sounds. He hears good. So now we have to teach him how to make sounds."

So that was really hard for him. It's really hard for one doctor to make a report like that to these higher-up staff. It's really hard, because they weren't there to see it for themselves. So they were just like St. Thomas, "Well, we have to be there to see it. You have to prove it to us." Well, if that happens, then they have to write to the higher regional directors. And that's even going to be more difficult. So he had a hard time making that report.

So we know how to perform that *iktomi* ceremony. You can use it for different things, like if you have a kid that is unruly, and you can't make him behave. Or you might have a kid that is destructive. If a person gets like that, you make twenty-seven yellow prayer ties and ask the spirit to change his character. Then that spirit will take care of it.

So when we went over to the East [Coast], there was this little boy there that was really unruly. He even jumped out of a window that was two stories high. He never broke his leg or anything. He just jumped. So he did things like that. He jumped on cars. He jumped off the roof of their barn. He crawled into holes, and wedged himself in there. You know, there would be big rocks there and tunnels. So he would wiggle himself in there, but then he couldn't wiggle back out. So he was stuck there. Then his parents couldn't find him. So that really scared his father and mother.

Then there was this big, heavy police dog lying there asleep. So he jumped on him. That police dog got scared and grabbed that kid by the neck. He shook him and was ready to kill him. Also, this unruly kid breaks things. If he doesn't want to eat anything, he just takes the plate and upsets it. Or if there is a picture, he'll tear it in half. He'll put ink on clothes. Or he takes a knife and cuts the tablecloth. So he does things like that.

His parents couldn't control him. They kept whipping him and scolding him. So that just drove him more crazy. Nothing they did to control him worked. So his parents were crying tears, "I'm really scared he's going to kill himself. I have begged him. I try not to whip him. I try to do everything. I give him everything he asks for, but he still does all these crazy things."

So I went and prayed. The spirit came. So he told me to make twenty-seven yellow ties and to leave them here. He told me the powers of the Four Winds were going to come and that they were going to recreate his mind. They were going to show him.

So, like, this kid watches cartoons and cartoons—Star Wars and those little crazy guys, like robots. Some fly in the air with those little guns. They jump up high and sail right through the air. So he sees those things. Then he wants to be one of those guys and fly around. He wants to put on a cape and jump high build-ings or lift a car or lift a man. So that got into his mind. So he was acting out those little, crazy things. So the spirit told us that those things he saw got embedded in his mind. It's like a little dart, or he gets a little cactus spine stuck on him and has to pull it out. The spirit interpreted it that way.

So the spirit said, "We are going to help. We are going to teach him what is real. He wants to reenact those feats or crimes or daring parts. He thinks those are real, but they are only colors and ink on paper or pictures drawn for a cartoon. So he got caught up there in his mind. So make those ties. We're spirits. We're real. We fly through the air. We can fly to any place. We go through walls. We could see and do anything. So we are going to educate him. We are going to show him the real thing. And we'll fix him."

So we went to the lodge. They had a stone-people-lodge there in the woods. So we went over there on a trail. Their house, garage, and barn stand there, and behind that is a meadow. So we have to cross that meadow. Then there's a bunch of big rocks, and the road curves. Then the lodge is there. The road keeps going, and there're bigger rocks, then the lakes. So that kid, he goes over those big boulders on the way there. When he sees a puddle of water, he just dives in there. Maybe it's just a shallow one, and he could bust his head open or break his neck. He does those things. It seemed like he couldn't think, so he does those daring things.

So we went to the lodge. The father and his boy went over to the lodge. His father heard some people hollering. So he men-tioned some guy's name and said, "I think that's him. That sounds like him."

So that boy said, "I'll go see. I think that is them."

"Did you see them coming?"

"No, but I think that's them."

So that boy took off running. So his father yelled at him, "You get back here. Come back over here. We'll both go. Don't run."

So he started following, but that boy was too fast for him. He ran over there and ran into those big rocks. His father was right behind him. All of a sudden, they saw all these creatures there with horns and tails like snakes. They were all lying there. They were talking and hollering. Then they started running towards them. So this kid stopped on those rocks and turned around. When he turned around, he started screaming and yelling and running. So his father yelled at him, "Stop. Stop." So he started chasing his boy again, but he couldn't catch him. That boy started running back to his house. So the father was about halfway through the meadow when that boy reached his house. That kid ran through the kitchen, through the dining room, and into the bedroom where his mother was. He fell right into her lap and started yelling, "Mama. Mama. I'll never go up there again. I'll never go up there. I'm going to behave. So please tell those spirits to leave me alone. I'll behave. I'll behave."

So then the father came in. What they saw out there were those creatures and those forms. They were all there hollering and yelling. So that kid saw the real of what he wanted to be. But when he saw the real ones, he got scared and took off. So while he was on the run, all that little tiny storm in his brain just blew away. It just vanished.

Later on his parents called. They called to tell us that their boy was all right. His mind was healed. So they thanked us. Then that boy wrote, and he thanked me, and he thanked the spirits. So later we went back there, and we saw him. He was totally different from what we had seen before. He was back to normal.

So we treat problems unexpectedly that way. I have no plan. I have no power. But when we prayed, the spirit came and suggested that. But we never know what they are going to do. So that's what they did. They corrected this boy's mind.

So I think we have to be careful how we train kids. We have too many cartoons and too many machine guns and robots that turn into a car, and the next thing they turn into an airplane. Those kinds of things. Those things puzzle your mind. Something that's good, they twist it around and turn it into a destructive monster. So their minds become all twisted that way. So we went into the lodge, and the spirit told us that those toy makers are misleading those kids. Once they see something bad, twenty-four hours later they reenact those crimes that they see. The spirit told us that.

So we help people in many different ways. That Chanunpa

carries help and health for everyone, and those spirits do unbelievable things. They can go anywhere and do anything. Like we had one boy whose father had a heart attack. He had a heart attack over in Madison, Wisconsin. So they rushed him to the hospital. He was in critical condition. So his boy was in Wichita, Kansas. He knew about the Chanunpa and our sacred ways. So he called me up in Denver and wanted to come over there. Instead of going to Wisconsin, he wanted to come over to Denver to help his father. So I told him to come on over. So they jumped in their van and started over there. I think it was about five hundred miles they had to drive. So on the way, while one guy was driving, the other guy was making tobacco ties, prayer ties. Then they changed drivers, and the other one started making ties. They had their Eagle Bundle—the 100 percent red virgin wool, eagle feather, eagle plume, and pink pearl conch—just like they saw it. So when they got there, we had everything ready.

So we went to the lodge. We had the wood and rocks piled up ready to light. We were just waiting for them to come there. As soon as they arrived, we started displaying the altar, putting up those robes and ties. Right away he filled the Chanunpa. Then he presented it to me. He offered that Chanunpa and said, "Tunkashila, I offer this Sacred Pipe." Then he stated his reason for the offering.

"My father is lying in the hospital with a heart attack. Tunkashila, I want to request that you go there and see my father. Please extend his life another day, another moon, another year, or another generation."

So he presented the Chanunpa four times. We learned that from the old people. You take this Chanunpa, and you pivot around one time. Then you present it. You do that four times. You state your reason for that presentation. So I held out my hands and took his offering. I took that Chanunpa.

So we went into the lodge, and the spirit came in. It was an eagle spirit. Then we told him about this boy's father and his heart attack. Then we sang four songs, and that eagle went over there to the hospital where his father was lying. I don't know how many miles it was to there, maybe a thousand or so miles. On the fourth song he came back in.

He said, "I touched him, and I fanned him. I gave him pure oxygen, and I gave him water. So you will see him four days from now."

Then he told us what was wrong with him. So he held his fist out and explained about five strands connecting in there. Then that unknown power came and attacked his blood. So that blood became like syrup and coagulated around the nerve. That caused the other parts to slip and weaken. So it slipped and locked. So I translated that for him. Then we said thank you, and that spirit left.

So what happened at the hospital was that that man was lying there. He was hooked up to all those bottles and tubes and wires and gadgets. He was sleeping. Then that spirit touched him. It electrified him, so he woke up. Later he told his wife how it happened to him.

He said, "Tunkashila touched my foot, and he woke me up. I saw him. He was standing there at the foot of my bed. He had a smile on his face, so I smiled, too. That touched my heart. Then he fanned me. Then he gave me water and left."

So after that happened there, he was like really awake. He felt really good. So he started pulling off all those wires and gadgets. He got up. He got out of bed. Then the doctor came in. I don't know whether he was smiling or not. He started saying, "You're sick. You're sick. You're dying. Get back in bed."

But this guy said, "No, I'm not sick. I'm all right."

So they hooked him back up to those little lights, and that little gadget there read that he was back to normal. So they took it off.

But they kept saying, "Are you sure you're all right?" They couldn't believe that he was dying one minute, and then the next minute he was up running around.

But he kept saying, "I'm all right. I'm all right."

So after we finished that lodge, we passed that sacred food around and finished up there. Then we went back to town. But on the way back, that boy still had a shadow of a doubt. So he wanted to call his father. He said, "Oh, stop here. There's a pay telephone." So we stopped. He got out and dropped money in there and started punching those buttons. He called that hospital. He asked them, "How's my dad?"

They told him, "Oh, he's up running around. He's ready to leave, but we want to hold him here to make sure he doesn't have any recurrences. We want to make sure that he's all right. Tomorrow he could go home."

So that boy went back home to Wichita. The next day his father went home from the hospital. His daughter was there, and she said, "You should fly to your son and see him."

He said, "Yeah, that's good. They were over there [in Denver], and they sent that eagle. That eagle came and touched me. So I'm going to see my son. I'm going to go say thank you."

So he flew over there to his son's home. That was on the fourth day. He didn't tell his son that he was coming. Just then that boy's phone rang.

"Son, pick us up. We're at the airport now. So come on over, and pick us up."

So they brought him back to the house. The first thing that he did was throw open his suitcase and brought out his Chanunpa. They prayed, and they smoked. So what the spirit told us came true. It was the fourth day, and that boy saw his father.

So unbelievable things like that happen. But you have to believe it first. Not wait until you see it first, then touch it, then believe it. Some people get that way. Then, if it doesn't happen, there is a lot of disappointment and discouragement. But you have to believe. You have to say it from the heart.

So those are the sacred ways of the Earth People and the sacred Chanunpa. I've lived with these powers all my life. I grew up with them. They are a part of me. They're real. They're the real science and technology. But over here we just drifted away for thousands of years. Now we need to come back to our roots. We need to come back to Grandfather, the Creator, and Grandmother, the Earth, where there is life everlasting.

So I want to end here with a prayer.

"Oh, Tunkashila, Grandfather, Great Spirit, we thank you ever so much for everything. Grandmother, we thank you for the nourishment and life you give us. Tunkashila, there are all kinds of sicknesses and all kinds of viruses floating around here.

Tunkashila, incurable sickness is floating around here and coming into our minds. Sometimes it comes and invades our bodies and destroys. There are pains and aches here, Tunkashila. But you are sacred. Your holy eyes see everything, Tunkashila. Let this wind blow [away] all these viruses and all these bad thoughts and bad words that come into our minds. Let it blow away piece by piece. Give us strength. Give us help and health, that way, Tunkashila. Continue to watch this sacred land and watch all of us. Continue to watch this Chanunpa and keep us from nuclear destruction. Tunkashila, I beg you and plead to you that you extend our life so that all my people will come together. Help us so we come to understand, so we keep you whole and keep you sacred. We come in a pitiful way, Tunkashila, so have mercy upon us. Have mercy on us so we have something to eat and something warm to wear this winter, Tunkashila. You're the only one who could do everything for us, Tunkashila. Help us that way. Grandmother, continue that way. Be with us, Tunkashila. You promised you'd be hovering over us all the time—you'd be in front; you'd be on both sides of us; you'd be in back of us; you'd be underneath us. Tunkashila, you promised that way. Let them understand that way, so whenever they need your help, Tunkashila, they'll look up to you. They'll ask for your help. Even if they don't ask you, Tunkashila, help them that way. So make them feel good. Make them happy. These beautiful people here, Tunkashila, keep them well that way. Ho, *mitakuye oyasin.*"

Glossary

altar. The specific arrangement of all the objects used in a ritual at the onset of the ceremony. Altar displays vary from ceremony to ceremony and shaman to shaman. Sometimes used to mean the Earth.

altar ceremony. Usually, a spirit-calling ceremony that is most often held in the room of a house; sometimes called a "Pipe ceremony." The shaman will display an altar that includes a Chanunpa. This ceremony is usually conducted in pitch darkness.

anpo wie. Lakota for the morning star (Venus). *Anpo* means "morning" or "dawn," and *wie* means "sun" or "star."

BIA. Bureau of Indian Affairs.

black light. Black light is pitch darkness, where the darkness is seen as the result of a force, not the absence of light. In Black Elk's view, there are two kinds of light.

catlinite. A soft stone mineral deposited at Pipestone, Minnesota, that is used by many Native Americans for carving the red stone bowls of their Sacred Pipes.

chahanpi. Lakota for sugar. *Cha* means "wood" or "tree," and *hanpi* means "tree sap."

Chanunpa. Lakota for the Sacred Pipe, often incorrectly referred to as the "peace pipe." *Cha* means "wood" or "tree" and *nunpa* means "two."

courage, patience, endurance, and alertness. In the Earth People philosophy, the four main personal virtues one must have in order to be able to handle the Chanunpa.

creeping-crawlers. In Black Elk's classification, all the creatures that live close to the ground in holes, such as snakes, lizards, ants, spiders, etc.

eagle-bone whistle. A single-note, ceremonial whistle usually made from the upper wing-bone (humerus) of an eagle.

Eagle Bundle. A ceremonial "robe" commonly used in the altar display that represents all the living creatures.

Eagle Nation. The eagles, whose function it is to control the weather. When sending prayers, Black Elk's phrase referring to the zenith direction.

Earth People. Black Elk's term for all human beings who live the fundamental, spirit/nature-based philosophy (his "Earth People philosophy") exemplified in earlier Native American cultures. Black Elk refers to himself as an "Earth Man."

fire, rock, water, and green. In the Earth People philosophy, the four basic constituents that go to form everything in existence.

fish-people. In Black Elk's classification, all the creatures that live in the water.

four-leggeds. In Black Elk's classification, all the quadrupeds.

Four Winds, Four Directions. The four cardinal points of the compass. The "power of the Four Winds" is the power over space. For example, if one wants to call in the spirit of a certain deceased relative, the shaman may call on the power of the Four Winds to seek out that spirit and bring it back to visit with relatives at the ceremony.

Grandfather. The male aspect of the Creator personified by wisdom, the sky, light, etc. Tunkashila.

Grandmother. The female aspect of the Creator personified by knowledge, the Earth, birth, etc.

hanbleceya. Lakota word referring to the vision quest ritual. *Hanble* means "to fast and attain vision," and *ceya* means "to cry or weep." In this case *ceya* is perhaps best translated as "to intensely pray for." Also, *hanble* comes from *han* (a noun contraction) for night and *ble,* referring to a quiet place or a lake. *Hanbleceya* is the ritual process by which a Lakota attempts to "catch" a spirit.

hecetu.   Lakota for "so be it" or "it is so."

heyoka.   Lakota word often translated as "clown." More correctly it refers to people who have had visions of the Thunder-Beings (bringers of lightning/thunder) and subsequently assume a routine form of conversation in which they say exactly the opposite of what they really mean. This socially acceptable behavior also extends to the person's actions, such as going naked outside in winter, "washing" in dirt, riding a horse facing to the rear, etc.

hogie-pogie.   Black Elk's rendition of "hodgie-podgie." He uses this phrase to refer to the illusionary tricks, the "hocus-pocus," of magicians.

hokshila.   Lakota for boy.

iktomi.   Lakota for spider; also, a folklore hero among the Lakota. Thus, *iktomi* is seen as a spirit power that can be called upon for healing, most notably to repair damaged nerves.

inipi.   The Lakota sweat-lodge (or stone-people-lodge) ceremony.

kinic-kinic, also kinnikkinnik or kinikinik [*sic*].   One of the plants used in Black Elk's Chanunpa smoking mixture; sometimes called "[red] bearberry" *(Arctostaphylos uva-ursi).*

Lakota.   The Native American language used by Black Elk's nation, the Oglala (Sioux) of the Rosebud and Pine Ridge reservations. Also, Black Elk and his people refer to themselves as the Lakota.

longhouse.   Usually, the rectangular-shaped religious ceremonial centers of the New England area, such as those of the Iroquois.

maka.   Lakota for Earth, earth, land, or ground.

medicine. The mysterious power inherent in the universe, not merely a prescribed drug. For example, there is good versus bad medicine; big versus little medicine; medicine water (whiskey); medicine people (plants used for healing); bear medicine (a ritual for specific applications of power); medicine dog (horse); elk medicine (for women), etc.

mitakuye oyasin. Lakota translated as "all my relations." This phrase is frequently uttered during ritual and is to remind people of their personal relatedness to everything that exists. It is spoken upon entering the stone-people-lodge; at the end of a personal prayer; when it is time to open the stone-people-lodge door; just after one has smoked the Chanunpa; and so forth.

mni. Lakota for water; comes from the root *ni,* meaning "one's breath or life."

pearl. A circular-cut piece of pink conch shell usually about one inch to two inches in diameter; often used in the display of an altar. It symbolizes the fish-people.

peta wicoicage. Lakota meaning "fire generation"; refers to the use of fire to shape and mold things.

robe. Black Elk's term for the body. "The deer laid down its robe" means the deer died. He also uses the term to refer to the rectangular pieces of colored cotton cloth used in the altar display. In ceremony, these six "robes" symbolize the major directions (powers) of the universe.

sacred bundle. Usually, an animal skin in which is wrapped the shaman's sacred instruments. Bundles might contain a single special medicine or several medicines. Sometimes bundles contain a singular sacred arrow, Sacred Pipe, or drum. Normally they contain sacred stones, feathers, plants, whistles, etc.

sacred food. Black Elk's phrase for the customary offering of food made at each ceremony in which water, corn, berries (chokecherries preferred), and meat are separately placed into four wooden bowls that are displayed on the altar. There is a special way to prepare this food, and it is often shared communally by all the participants during the close of a ceremony.

Sacred Pipe. A ritual instrument commonly used by Native Americans. It usually consists of an elbow-shaped stone bowl connected to a wooden stem. It is used mainly for consecrating actions and communicating with the spirits. Black Elk considers it to be the most holy implement in the world. See Chanunpa.

seven fireplaces. The seven basic sacred ceremonies used by the Lakota Nation. Also the Seven Council Fires, or branches, of the Teton Dakota.

shina. Lakota for blanket or robe. This is the Lakota word Black Elk uses for the sacred robes used in his altar display.

stone-people-lodge. Black Elk's preferred term for the Lakota sweat-lodge purification ceremony.

taku wakan. Lakota for sacred mystery. Also means something powerful.

tezi. Lakota for stomach or womb. Black Elk speaks of the stone-people-lodge as being the *tezi* of Grandmother, where we come to be reborn.

Thunder Spirits, Thunder-Beings. Powerful spirits that live in the West. When these spirits come, one usually sees lightning and/or hears thunder. Black Elk's power comes mainly from these spirits.

tobacco root. Usually, the root of the lovage or osha plant (*Ligusticum* [most species]), which is one of the plants used in Black Elk's Chanunpa smoking mixture.

tobacco tie, prayer tie. A one-inch square of cotton cloth into which a pinch of tobacco is placed as a prayer is offered forth. The cloth is then twisted shut and tied onto a string. These strings of "prayers" are then used as part of the altar display. Black Elk usually requires two such strings to display his altar, one consisting of 150 ties and the other of 50 ties.

toka. Lakota for enemy. Black Elk often uses this word when referring to the agent causing a sickness. To "cure" means to remove the *toka*.

Tree of Knowledge. In the Earth People philosophy, all the knowledge that goes to form nature. Grandmother is the knowledge. That which we discover via science. One aspect of the Tree of Life.

Tree of Life. All the people and their interactions with the creation. If people follow the "Red Road," a spiritual-based life, the Tree of Life will bloom, and the people will prosper. If they follow the "Black Road," a material-based life, the tree will wither.

tunkan tipi. Lakota expression used by Black Elk to refer to the stone-people-lodge. *Tun* means "birth," *kan* means "age," and *tipi* means "house."

Tunkashila. Lakota referring to the Grandfather or male aspect of the Creator. Best translated in English as "God." (Pronounced: Toon-kash'-she-la.)

Turtle Island. The Western Hemisphere (North and South America).

two-leggeds. Human beings, or spirits that come in the guise of human beings.

vision quest. A widespread, Native American tradition in which mainly males seek personal visions via isolation and ritual action. This is the primary means by which Lakota shamans obtain, over time, their medicine powers.

wakan. Lakota for holy.

washicu. Lakota for white man. (Pronounced: waa-she'-chew.)

White Buffalo Maiden, also the Buffalo-Calf Maiden. In Lakota history, the spirit woman that brought the first Chanunpa to them, made from the leg bone of a buffalo calf.

winged-people. In Black Elk's classification, all the creatures that fly, be they mammal (bat), insect, or bird.

wisdom, knowledge, power, and gift. In the Earth People philosophy, the successive operational levels of cosmic forces that give rise to all that exists. For example, the "rules of nature" would be included here as well as the "ways of the Creator." Black Elk also uses the words *love* and *talent* as synonyms for *gift*. (As humans, we receive only one drop of each.)

yuwipi.   A specific Lakota spirit-calling ceremony in which the shaman is bound tightly in a blanket and subsequently released by the spirits during their visitation. This ceremony has a wide range of applications for help and health.